THE POWER OF
PRAISE
AND
WORSHIP

by
Terry Law

VICTORY HOUSE PUBLISHERS
Tulsa, Oklahoma

Unless otherwise identified, all Scripture quotations are taken from the *King James Version* of the Bible.

Scripture quotations marked NASB are from the *New American Standard Bible*, copyright © The Lockman Foundation 1960, 1962, 1963, 1968, 1971, 1972, 1973, 1975, 1977. Used by permission.

THE POWER OF PRAISE AND WORSHIP
ISBN 0-932081-01-0
Copyright © 1985 by Terry Law
Terry Law Ministries
P. O. Box 92
Tulsa, Oklahoma 74101

Published by Victory House, Inc.
P. O. Box 700238
Tulsa, Oklahoma 74170

Editorial assistance by Stephen R. Clark

Contents

Dedicated to Jan

a loving wife
a devoted mother
my best friend

Your life here and in heaven
inspired this book.

INTRODUCTION

I praise God for Terry Law, one of the most God-gifted men of God I've ever known.

Terry was led to attend Oral Roberts University by an angel and through a dedicated layman. At ORU he shone like a new star, becoming an outstanding student and leader. He graduated into a worldwide ministry of signs and wonders of the gospel, particularly behind the iron curtain in communist nations.

Terry has touched, and is touching, hundreds of thousands across America as well.

When he ministers with us he carries God's anointing and is a living example, and leader, in "The Power of Praise and Worship."

Oral Roberts

Oral Roberts

1

Healing Encounter Through Praise

The premise of this book is very simple. *Praise and worship brings us healing and deliverance.* Yet, as simple as this concept is, most believers have never grasped the profound impact of the reality of this truth. They know intuitively in their minds that it's true, yet they've never applied the truth to their lives. They've not fully believed it in their hearts.

Until a few years ago, I, too, did not fully comprehend this simple concept. But, after years of overseas ministry and character shaping experiences, all of which culminated with an overwhelming personal tragedy, God revealed to me the power of this simple truth. *Praise and worship brings us healing and deliverance.*

You do not need to wait for years, as I did, to begin to understand and experience the power of this concept. *The power of praise and worship is available to you and all believers now! Today* you can begin to experience healing and deliverance in every area of your life as you follow and apply the principles I am going to share with you.

This book is the result of two years of intense, exhaustive study in God's Word. And every principle has been applied and proven true in personal experience.

Thousands of people around the world can testify positively that *praise and worship brings us healing and deliverance.* There are thousands who are living examples of the miracle-working power of God that is released through praise and worship.

Yet, there are multiplied thousands more who have failed to fully realize God's power and how to access His healing and deliverance in their lives. Even those who were born and raised in Bible-believing churches have missed out on God's power. I know this is true because I was a preacher's kid! Let me share a small part of my story to illustrate how God led me into the powerful revelation of this message.

Resisting God's call

I grew up in Canada. My father was a minister with the Pentecostal Assemblies of Canada (Assemblies of God). He was a pioneer pastor, establishing new churches in the difficult areas of northern Saskatchewan. My father played the guitar, and my mother played the accordion, and together spread the gospel.

From the age of 2½ years, I was always independent. As a child, I often would dream of heading off for "the wide open spaces." At age 9, I had my own paper route, earning all my own spending money, buying my own clothes, and so on. By age 16, I was working in a grocery store and earning as much money as my father was in the ministry; I was able to buy my own car.

I was very independent and self-sufficient. I didn't want to have to rely on anyone for my survival. And, seeing the hardships my mom and dad had to endure, I did not want anything to do with the ministry. I wanted to go my own way in life. But God had a different plan.

When I was 13, we went to Vancouver Island for a campmeeting. One night in the service, I was very moved by the message. Later, after everyone else had gone back to their cabins, I sat alone in the meeting room, in the darkness, praying.

Dwight McClaughlin, the speaker, awoke in the middle of the night remembering that he'd left his Bible on the platform. He got up and came back to retrieve it. When he came into the room, he called out, "Is anybody there?" I replied simply, "Yes." He walked over to me in the darkness, laid his hands on my shoulders, and began to pray for me.

Soon, as the Spirit of God began to move upon him, he began to prophesy over me. "Young man," he said, "I see you standing before hundreds of thousands of people as you preach the gospel all around the world."

I began to tremble and shake all over. An anointing came upon my life then, even though I was too young to really understand it. The next night, Rev. McClaughlin called me forward and explained to the audience what had happened. From that time on, I felt like a marked man inside. I was called, but I didn't want to go.

After graduating from high school, I entered university to study law. My intention was to become a lawyer and go into politics. I had no desire for the ministry.

One Sunday afternoon, some university friends and I got drunk. We got it into our heads to go to my father's church and disrupt the service. There was a guest minister that evening. We sat in the back pew, talking out loud, laughing, creating a disturbance. But no one paid any attention to us. The ushers ignored us, and so did the speaker.

About half-way through the service, a spirit of conviction came upon me and I became instantly sober.

God spoke in my heart, and said, "This is the night. I want you." I knew what it meant. And I knew I could not resist God any longer. I went forward and committed my life to the Lord. This was in 1960. Three days later, I left law school and entered Bible college.

It took three years to graduate from Bible college. I was working in a hardware store and was desperately seeking God's direction. One Sunday after the church service, I went into the prayer room and a spirit of intercession came upon me. One of the assistant pastors prayed with me. We were there for four hours before I felt a release.

I had been praying in my prayer language, and the pastor told me what I had been praying. I had been praying the words of Isaiah 6:5, "Woe is me! for I am undone; because I am a man of unclean lips, and I dwell in the midst of a people of unclean lips: for mine eyes have seen the King, the Lord of hosts." My victory and release came as I had prayed in the Spirit verse 8, ". . . Whom shall I send, and who will go for us? Then said I, Here am I; send me." I knew I was to go, but I didn't know where.

As I left the church, and stepped outside into the cold November air, God spoke in my heart. He said, "You're going to travel with Dennis Bjorgan."

Dennis and I had grown up together in Prince Albert, Saskatchewan. We had been very close friends. His family was very musical, and I knew he wanted to travel in ministry. But I didn't know where he was. I hadn't heard from Dennis for over a year.

The next morning, I received a letter from Dennis that had taken a month to reach me. He stated that he felt God wanted us to travel together! That's all I needed. I bought a bass guitar and amplifier, and Dennis taught me to play. We travelled throughout Canada and the northern United States singing and preaching God's Word.

Always having had a heart for foreign missions, in 1965 we felt impressed to go to Africa. So, we raised some money, and took a freighter from Montreal to Capetown. We spent 28 days on the ocean. We were only 21 years old with virtually no money. Yet we spent the year in Africa, and saw thousands accept Christ.

Called to learn

The next year, 1966, Dennis married and we stopped our music ministry. I took the pastorate of a small church in a small Canadian town near my father's church. My congregation was 25 people, and I was with them for about two years.

It was during this time that Oral Roberts brought his crusade to Edmonton, and I went to hear him. It was September, 1967, and I was very impressed with Bro. Roberts. Following the service one night, I passed a literature table and picked up a brochure on a new school called Oral Roberts University. As soon as I picked it up, I knew I was to go there.

Again, I began to resist the Lord. I didn't want to go back to school. I felt I had enough education, and I was ready to get started in my world ministry. I fought it for three months, but finally yielded.

One day I was working with a friend, Ed Stahl, on his ranch. We were putting up a new fence line, and I told him that I had decided to go to ORU. He stopped, dropped the fence post he was holding, and just stared at me. He told me to get in his truck. We drove out to the center of his ranch, and he stopped and pointed to a place near a hill.

He said, "Three months ago an angel of the Lord appeared to me right over there. He told me you would be going to ORU, and when you made up your mind I was to see that all your needs were taken care of." We sat in the truck and cried.

Marriage and international ministry

Three months later, I was at ORU. I was awestruck with the campus. But, after a few weeks I became frustrated not being able to preach. I stayed awake one night praying, telling the Lord how much I wanted to do something. The next morning I was asked to become involved in Oral Robert's meetings, and six weeks after I'd started at ORU, I was leading the song service for Oral Roberts in his West Palm Beach crusade. Working with Roberts began to stretch my thinking and enlarge my vision.

The next spring, I was sent to Europe with a World Action Team. It was on this tour that I met my wife, Jan D'Arpa. Our first close encounter came on a sightseeing trip in London, and our first date was on a mission to Israel. She was a student at ORU from Tampa, and 2½ weeks after we first dated I knew I would marry her.

Before we were married, I explained to Jan about my call and my eventual worldwide ministry. I asked her if she could really deal with such a life, knowing I'd be away much of the time. For two weeks, she prayed about it, and then told me that she was fully supportive of my ministry. We were married in Tampa on January 21, 1969.

The following month, in February, we formed Living Sound at ORU. We intended this to be a weekend music ministry. The co-founder of the ministry was my friend, Larry Dalton, who is blessed with a great musical gift. At our very first concert, in a charismatic Baptist church in Kansas City, I received a word from the Lord. Living Sound would go to Africa.

I was shocked, but knew this was the Lord's will. Each member had to decide for themselves if they would go, and only one decided against it. We raised the funds we needed and applied for visas.

Little did I know what kind of an ordeal we were in for. Our visas were at first rejected. We had to change our plans and go to Rhodesia instead of South Africa. In Rhodesia, we were turned away at the airport for no apparent reason. We spent three frustrating weeks in Mozambique trying to get into Rhodesia, and finally were "deported" to New York. We were totally discouraged and confused, and all our money was gone.

Our friends, the Cardones in Philadelphia arranged for us to stay at a Teen Challenge center as we tried to rethink our dilemma. There, we received a special word of encouragement, and were told that our visas were clear for South Africa.

An airline company extended us round trip passage for our entire group, and we finally made it into South Africa. We ministered there for a year, and, during one of our services, the Lord called me into the Soviet Bloc. Living Sound had entered into the beginning of international evangelism that would ultimately affect entire countries.

Growth and problems

Over the next several years, the ministry grew, and so did my family. We had three children between 1970 and 1980—Misty, Scot and Rebecca. During this time, Jan never complained about the pressures of the ministry, and never argued with me over my decisions. She was a tremendous mother.

Living Sound ministered throughout Africa, Europe, the Carribean, and the Orient. Soon, we grew to two groups, then three, then four groups singing all over the world. We went into Poland, Yugoslavia, Rumania, Hungary and finally the U.S.S.R.

As the organization grew, so did the pressures. Our finances were always marginal. Running the operation from the road was difficult, so we established a small central office in Tulsa, Oklahoma. In 1981, we began to experience severe stress within the organization.

By early 1982, because of a business recession, our giving receipts had dropped more than fifty percent. Having no practical business experience or training, I felt fully the pressures. I knew I was responsible for the organization's needs. I felt like I was walking in a fog as I fought to resolve the problems.

During this time, I always was the last one to take salary. For three months, I drew no income. One day, I came home from a series of meetings, and found Jan crying in the kitchen because we had no food. I tried to comfort and reassure her, telling her that God would provide, and then I left for a meeting at our office. When I returned, my daughter Misty was dancing and laughing in the house. I asked Jan what was going on and she handed me an envelope with ten one hundred dollar bills in it.

Our son's baseball coach had driven up to our gate, handed the envelope to Scotty and told him to give it to his mom. We didn't even know the man personally, and there was no way he could have known our situation. I called the man and thanked him, and we all praised God for providing.

Inspite of this, I still felt tremendous guilt over what was happening in my family and the organization. I was thirty-nine years old and felt I should be doing a better job providing for my family and in running the ministry.

That summer, I called in three Christian businessmen in Tulsa who were friends. I explained my problems and gave them full authority to examine the ministry and recommend changes so that we could survive. I agreed to follow their advice.

What they came back with was hard to take. I had to let go over half of our Living Sound staff, as well as radically alter my own management style. There was nothing more painful than having to tell friends that they were no longer working for me.

These measures really tore up the ministry. It looked as if we were virtually falling apart. We had mortgaged everything we could to the maximum just to keep afloat. My close friend decided to leave for another ministry. It was a very difficult time for me personally. I actually began to wonder if I was coming to the end of my ministry.

Tragedy and crisis

That fall, September, 1982, I had to go to London for a series of board meetings with the trustees of our European corporation. Just before leaving from Kennedy airport, I called Jan to tell her good-bye. I hadn't seen her for a few days as I had been in services in North Carolina.

I arrived in London on Tuesday morning and we were in meetings all day. David Weir had come with me from Tulsa. By that evening I was exhausted, and went to bed around 9:30. At 11:00 p.m., David shook me awake. "What's the matter?" I asked groggily.

I wasn't prepared for what he was about to tell me.

"Terry," he began, "I have some terrible news. We just got a call from Tulsa. *Jan has been killed in a car accident.*"

For ten minutes, I just sat there in bed stunned, not moving. Then, I said that it was all a dream and I would go back to sleep, when I woke up, it would be OK. But it was no dream. *My wife was dead.* Thirty minutes later I was on the phone, telling my children that their mommy was gone.

I felt tremendous guilt for not being there with them. And for not having been there for Jan, even though I could have done nothing for her. That night I grieved, I cried, I questioned God. The next day, flying home, I prayed and cried, and told God over a hundred times that I was through with the ministry. There was no way I could go on alone.

Jan died on September 28, 1982. Two days later, October 1, we had her funeral. My pastor, Billy Joe Daughterty, spoke, as did Oral Roberts, and Kenneth Hagin, Jr. prayed. People from all over the world had flown in. During the service, the Spirit of God came upon me and I began to prophesy about my ministry. The Spirit indicated through me that I was not done, that the vision was still alive in my heart. But that's not the way I felt. Personally, I was in spiritual collapse. I was numb.

Following the funeral, I couldn't pray. I became angry and bitter toward the Lord. I blamed Him for letting Jan die. After all I had done and endured for the gospel, I thought this was terribly unfair to me. Later, I realized I was angry at the wrong person. God did not cause my wife's death.

But still, at the time, I was confused and hurt. About three weeks after the funeral, Oral Roberts called and asked me to come to his office. He had just lost a son in Tulsa, and we sat, talking about our pain.

After about two hours, Oral stood up, pointed his finger at me, and said, "Terry, I'm going to tell you something that could save your life if you do what I say." I knew he was referring to my spiritual life and was eager to hear anything helpful. "Go home, get down on your knees, and start to pray in the spirit. You have got to begin to praise the Lord."

I was flabbergasted. How could I do that? I hurt. I was numb. I felt nothing. "I can't," I protested.

But Oral was insistent, "You *have* to, Terry. You *have* to."

The necessity of praise and worship

The next morning, my alarm went off before day-break. I knelt by my bed and tried to enter into praise. It was one of the most excruciating spiritual experiences of my life. The inner pain seemed unbearable. I said the word "Hallelujah". It sounded hollow. It echoed in the room. I said "I praise you Lord." My thoughts began to taunt me.

It was the Devil who answered me. "Terry Law you are a hypocrite. How can you praise God after He killed your wife." The Devil was sowing lies in my mind. "You don't really mean those words," he said. "You're lying!"

It is difficult to describe in words what I felt. I actually believed the enemy. How could I praise the Lord when I felt this bitterness and anger inside? I was so tempted to give up. Time passed slowly. Fifteen minutes seemed like a life time.

Gradually, I came to a moment of truth. I knew I

had to make a decision. The words of Psalm 34:1 came to me. "I will bless the Lord at all times: his praise shall continually be in my mouth." Spiritually, I was looking into a dark abyss of despair and self pity. I felt that I had good reason to feel sorry for myself. Hadn't I risked my life for God time and again on mission fields all over the world. It just wasn't fair.

The words came again, "I will bless the Lord at all times: his praise shall continually be in my mouth." The devil answered, "you might as well give up - there's no hope. God has failed you."

Then I decided. I said out loud, "Lord, I will bless you at all times. Lord, I will bless you at all times." Something happened way down inside my spirit. I had taken the last step toward God. But the Devil does not give up easily. He taunted me again. "When you praise God that way, you're lying. You don't mean those words. How can you?" I said it louder, "Lord, I bless you at all times." The battle was on.

I waited for some kind of emotional release, some kind of inner help from God, but it didn't come. I was acting on sheer willpower alone. I was praising the Lord in obedience to His Word without assistance from my feelings. I praised for thirty minutes ... then an hour ... then an hour and a half ... then two hours. I still felt nothing.

Sometime between two and two and a half hours, I felt a pressure building up inside. It was like water building up behind a dam. I kept praising. It felt like the dam would explode. Then it did. With a mighty rush, I began to cry with hot stinging tears. My shoulders began to heave. It was like a cramp in my stomach had suddenly released. I raised my hands.

How many hours I was on my knees, I don't remember. The spirit of prophecy came on me and I began to prophesy my own healing. I felt the Holy Spirit take the oil of healing and pour it over my fractured, torn emotions. I was being healed. Obedience in praise and worship had brought healing to my inner man.

Since that time, I've shared this message of hope with others, and repeatedly, they too have experienced the same healing and deliverance. You see it was through the power of praise and worship that I found healing and deliverance in all areas of my life—emotional, spiritual, physical, psychological.

This concept has reshaped my entire ministry. It has revolutionized my life. And if you'll apply the principles as I share them with you, you too will experience spiritual renewal. What Oral Roberts told me, I'm now saying to you.

If you will begin to praise and worship God as He wants you to, healing and deliverance is yours *right now!* This book will show you how to open your life to God so that you can see His miracle-working power released in your situation *today!*

2
God's Dynamic Directive

I always have believed the words that Jesus spoke to His disciples in Mark 16:17, 18b, when He said, "And these signs shall follow them that believe; In my name shall they cast out devils; they shall speak with new tongues . . . they shall lay hands on the sick, and they shall recover." This instruction is very clear. We are to lay hands on the sick and they are to recover. This is to be the proclamation we make to a world of needy people.

When I came to Oral Roberts University, I was invited to travel with Oral Roberts in his crusade ministry. This was in 1968 when his crusades were winding down. Six weeks after I arrived at O.R.U., I was traveling with Roberts. I led the crusade song services. I helped pray for the sick. I watched the manifestation of the power of God in this man's ministry.

I had not seen many powerful manifestations of healing power in my own ministry in Canada, and as I stood in the healing lines night after night, I was amazed to see miracles take place right before my eyes.

Yet, I still struggled with a great faith barrier. This was possible for Oral Roberts, for he was such a great man. But it simply was not possible for me. I believed I did not have the spiritual credentials that I should have. I was filled with a sense of inferiority when it came to moving by faith into the fact that a healing ministry could be manifested in my own life.

But, deep down inside me, there always was a prayer to the Lord, "Father, use me in this way. Help me to bring your healing power to people who are sick and who need deliverance."

A mandate from the Holy Spirit

Following the trauma of my wife's death, and after being counseled by Oral Roberts, I moved into a new relationship with God in terms of praise and worship. I entered a dimension in praying and flowing in the Holy Spirit that I had not known previously in my life. There were days when I spent many hours praying in the Spirit and living in close harmony with the Lord.

About two months after my wife's passing, and following Roberts' instruction to move into praise and worship, I was praying in my room at home. I had been praying for over an hour in the spirit when I sensed the spirit of prophecy coming upon me.

I began to speak out what the Holy Spirit was giving to my spirit. I prayed in a very unusual manner. In fact, I prayed what was to become a divine mandate for my ministry. The Holy Spirit spoke through me, and said, *"I am going to have you bring salvation, healing, and deliverance to people everywhere through the message of praise and worship."*

I always have been very cautious when people say they have a prophetic word from the Lord. I have seen many make mistakes in this area. But this time, I was absolutely sure God was speaking to me. However, *I had difficulty connecting healing and deliverance with a message of praise and worship.* I did not know anyone who ministered healing and deliverance to people through the message of praise and worship. The two were in my opinion, mutually exclusive.

After the Lord spoke to me in this manner, I spent several hours meditating on the message. I struggled with how to put the two concepts together. What did healing and deliverance have to do with praise and worship? Praise and worship is ministry to God. Healing and deliverance is ministry to people.

What was the connection I had never seen before? Why hadn't the great healing evangelists discovered this? I had never seen Oral Roberts minister healing to the sick through praise and worship. Neither did other great evangelists who minister throughout America and in other parts of the world. What was the Holy Spirit leading me into?

However, my reaction to this word from the Lord was immediate. That day, I called our Living Sound office and told my Executive Director, Don Moen, what had happened in my devotions. I said, "The new direction of our ministry is going to be one of praise and worship." I instructed him to take all of the music lead sheets that Living Sound had used for thirteen years, and to examine their theme content.

I knew we were going to have to be single-minded in presenting a message of praise and worship to the people. Any of our songs that were not exclusively praise and worship would have to be set aside. This did not mean that our previous music was wrong. Only that there is a time and place for everything in every ministry.

I was convinced that we were to go in one direction primarily; that we should be single-minded in our approach. We had to set aside approximately ninety percent of the music we had been singing.

I took the next step of faith and we began to print posters and flyers promoting praise and healing crusades. This was a great step of faith for me. I did not know the mechanics of my message. I did not even have a theological background for it at that point. I simply knew that my response to God must be immediate obedience, and so we began to book our first series of crusades for February of 1983.

As I prepared myself for that first crusade meeting, I went to the Word. I prayed, asking the Lord for spiritual insight concerning healing, deliverance, salvation, and the message of praise and worship. *I knew this was what God wanted, and yet I didn't know how to present the message.*

In my times of prayer, reading the Bible, and extensive times of fasting, I began to see some principles emerging from Scripture. I also began to remember experiences from my ministry over the years, and *suddenly things that happened many years before began to make sense for the first time.*

Evidence from the past

I began my university training at Oral Roberts University in January of 1968. In that spring semester, the school decided to send a World Action Team to Europe for summer ministry. I was asked to travel with the team and play an instrument, and also to speak in our meetings overseas.

During our tour in Europe, three days opened up in our schedule. Our leaders decided it would be good to travel out of Finland to minister in Estonia for those three days. Estonia is one of fifteen Soviet socialist republics, and is located immediately across the Baltic from Helsinki, Finland.

One night a young man from the underground church came to our hotel. His name was Jaanus Karner. The underground church met illegally and was not a part of the registered church in the city. Jaanus asked if four young men from our group would come with him to one of their secret meetings being held that evening. I quickly agreed to go.

When we left the hotel lobby, we had to leave our passports at the desk. There was a man standing in the lobby. It was very obvious who he was. He had a raincoat on with the collar pulled up around his ears, and was wearing sunglasses in the dark of night. As we left the lobby and crossed the street to the bus stop, the man followed behind us.

When the bus stopped, Jaanus whispered that we were not to move until he did. We stood on the sidewalk waiting. The back door of the bus was open, and as the bus revved its engines to leave, Jaanus said, "Now!", and we jumped onto the bus at the last moment. We left the man following us standing on the sidewalk.

We went several blocks on the bus, got off, caught a cab, and then criss-crossed the city for about half an hour. We got out of the taxi, walked the last mile to an apartment building, and up to the second floor into a room that was totally dark. I remember stumbling over someone's leg when I walked in through the door, and sensing that the room was full.

We sat in darkness for approximately one hour. At one point a truck stopped outside and someone moved to the curtain, pulling it aside, wondering if the police had arrived.

When the lights finally were turned on, Jaanus came out from a back room holding some manuscripts he was translating into the language of his people. I remember looking at Jaanus, close up. I could see the fire of commitment burning in his eyes as he showed us the various manuscripts.

For the first time in my life, I recognized the lack of my own commitment to Jesus. I'd never had to place my faith on the line. I had never been in a position where my life was threatened by what I believed, but I knew that Jaanus had.

I knew that the police had invaded his home on three different occasions. He had been beaten. He had been expelled from university for his faith in Christ. He had paid a tremendous price. As I looked at him, I prayed a silent prayer, *"Lord, if you ever call me to bring the Gospel to these people, I promise that I will do it, no matter what the cost."*

It was a prayer prayed in a moment of emotion, like a foxhole prayer. It didn't take long for me to forget I had even prayed the prayer. But I have learned that my prayers and my vows to God are never to be taken lightly. You and I may forget our prayers, but God does not.

Called by His voice

This truth was graphically illustrated for me two years later. In 1969, I formed the musical group called Living Sound. From the very beginning of the ministry we felt directed toward missions overseas. In 1970, we traveled to southern Africa to minister for one year. There were sixteen of us; myself, eight vocalists, and seven musicians.

We were committed to presenting a salvation message, and our ministry was very successful. Three months into the tour in March, the group was singing in a church about 60 miles outside of Johannesburg. While they were singing, I went into a prayer room immediately behind the platform. I placed my Bible on the floor, and was kneeling on the rug, reading my text and praying, preparing myself to preach.

As I knelt in prayer, I sensed an unusual presence in the room. I knew I was in the presence of the Lord. Then He spoke to me. I did not see Him, but I heard Him speak in an audible voice. I not only heard the voice with my ears, but my entire body vibrated to the sound. The Lord said, *"I am going to send you into the Soviet Bloc. You will do things there that most people will believe impossible. If you obey and trust me, I will protect you."*

I had forgotten what I'd prayed two years earlier as I looked into Jaanus' eyes. Neither had I been thinking about the Soviet Bloc. When this word from the Lord came to me, I was overwhelmed. My first reaction was, *"No!* I don't want to go. Lord, please call someone else. This demands too great a commitment. The price is too high!"

I argued for the next several moments with the Lord. I had been in the Soviet Bloc. I knew the oppression and danger there, and I did not want to obey the call to go back. I was deeply agitated in my spirit. I was stretched out on the floor, trembling, perspiring, and filled with fear.

The team finished their music in the auditorium and I knew it was time to preach. I picked up my Bible, and walked out of the room. One of the young men on the team, Jim Gilbert, said to me later, "When you walked out of that room, you looked as if you had seen a ghost. Your face was white, your lips were trembling."

I walked to the pulpit, put my Bible on it, opened to my text, and tried to read the Scripture. I was unable to say a word. I made several attempts to read my text. I was standing there in rebellion, unwilling to submit myself to His call. Finally, I had to surrender. I stood in front of the crowd, approximately six to eight hundred people, and told them that God had called us that night, to minister in the Soviet Bloc.

A concert for communists

I told the Lord I would not solicit any invitations to go to a Soviet Bloc country, and if He wanted us to get there, the invitation would have to come through His leading and direction. For two years, nothing happened, but this didn't bother me at all.

In June of 1972, a letter came from Poland inviting us to sing on the campus of the Jagiellonian University in Krakow, Poland. The letter appeared to be written by University students who wanted us to sing for a special student event on campus. The letter was written in broken English, and it was difficult deciphering exactly what they meant. But it did seem clear that they wanted us to sing for them in October, that fall.

Our overseas schedule had us traveling in Europe, so in October, we traveled into Krakow. When we arrived in the city, we made contact with our sponsors. Soon I realized something was terribly wrong.

These were not just University students as we had thought, although some were students. These were the leaders of the Youth Communist Party, called the People's Party in southern Poland, and they had understood that Living Sound was an American rock-and-roll group. They had scheduled us for two fund-raising benefits in the headquarters of the Communist Youth Party. I was horrified, but I did not tell them we were a

Christian singing group. I told them we did all kinds of music.

When we went to set up our equipment, some of the communist youth tried to buy drugs from us. The first concert was at five o'clock, the next one at seven. The room filled with about two hundred youth. The ceiling was low, and the room was blue with smoke. Beer bottles were on every table. It was not what you'd expect at a Christian concert! Everyone in the room was a card-holding member of the Communist Party. This was their private club.

After three songs in our first concert, I could tell the audience was becoming quite upset. I got up, and whispered a silent prayer. I knew why the Lord had brought us to this place at this time, but still, I was hesitant to move in the anointing of the Holy Spirit I knew was upon me.

Finally, I began to preach. I explained that Marx and Lenin did not have the way. There was only One who was the way, and His name was Jesus Christ. I explained what Christ had done in the life of each one in the Living Sound team, and in my life, particularly. I shared how Jesus Christ had come into my heart and changed me from a sinner into a child of God. I then explained how Christ could do the same thing for them.

In my closing statement, I challenged them to turn from Communism and to respond to Jesus Christ. When I finished, there was absolute quiet in the room.

I walked off the stage, where two young men were waiting behind the curtains. They escorted me into the basement. They took me to a room where four others were seated at a table. They were very angry. They cursed, and demanded to know who had sent us. They accused us of being connected with the Central Intelligence Agency (C.I.A.).

I spent, at least, 45 minutes in the basement, fearing at any moment that I would be hauled off to jail and never see the West again. Finally, the leader spoke to me, and said, "Listen, we are embarrassed by what you have done here, but we have taken in much money for both of the concerts and we do not want to give it back. We cannot allow you to say anything more, but the group must continue to sing for the audience."

I agreed, and was allowed to go back upstairs. By this time the team was beginning the second concert. They had been very concerned, and when they saw me standing at the back of the auditorium, a smile of relief showed on several faces. But they realized, too, that they were on their own.

Halfway through the second concert, I sensed the anointing of the Holy Spirit come into the room. Our singers began to raise their hands in praise and worship to the Lord. Several of them were crying as they stood in the presence of the Lord. I looked around the room and was amazed. The communist youth were electrified by what they were watching.

Their Communist ideology did not allow them to believe in God, yet here was a group of American and Canadian young people worshipping someone who did not exist! This was the most powerful testimony we could have given these people. From that moment on, the atmosphere in the club changed.

Near the end of the concert, the group sang "God is moving by His Spirit, Moving through all the earth, Signs and wonders when God moves, Move oh Lord, in me." When the strains of the song died away, there was a long moment of absolute quiet, and then in one body, the audience stood to their feet, and they began to applaud. They clapped in unison, and it was thunderous. Then they demanded encore after encore. We were there until 3:30 a.m. leading many into a personal relationship with Jesus Christ.

As we left the Communist club to go back to the dormitory where we were staying, I knew I had witnessed one of the most significant events of my life. *The power of God had been manifested through praise and worship in a way I had never before seen.* I didn't understand why it worked. I just knew that it did work.

In subsequent ministry in Soviet countries, especially Poland and the U.S.S.R., we saw more demonstrations of the power of God manifested through praise in our music.

I discovered that if we would worship God before our audiences, no matter how hostile they were, through the praise and worship we would literally bind the powers and forces that oppressed them. The people then became susceptible to the Gospel and to the anointing of the Holy Spirit that was upon us through our praise and worship.

Armed for spiritual warfare

These were the experiences I recalled as I pondered the divine mandate that the Holy Spirit had given me to, "... *bring salvation, healing, and deliverance to people everywhere through the message of praise and worship.*"

As I meditated on these past events and my present directive, I began to analyze the elements: What happened in times of praise and worship? Why did people become so open to the Spirit? Why did they more readily respond to the message of the Gospel? Then the insight came: *spiritual warfare.*

Communism, Capitalism, Socialism, and other so-
cial, and even religious philosophies are more than
mere ideologies. Each system has operating within it a
spirit. And the nature of the spirit determines the nature of the philosophy.

We have ministered in Moscow, and several Soviet
Bloc countries many times. I've often been interrogated
by the KGB. And as I thought about each of these experiences, the spirit behind Communism became easily
recognizable: *Satan.*

As I continued to pray and meditate on these
things, and the Spirit's directive concerning praise and
worship, a single word kept repeating in my mind,
"Strongholds . . . strongholds . . . strongholds . . ." I
knew Paul had used this word in his writings somewhere in the Bible, and so I looked it up in my concor-
dance and turned to it in 2 Corinthians 10:3-5:

> 3 For though we walk in the flesh, we do not war
> after the flesh:
> 4 (For the weapons of our warfare are not carnal,
> but mighty through God to the pulling down of
> strongholds;)
> 5 Casting down imaginations, and every high thing
> that exalteth itself against the knowledge of God,
> and bringing into captivity every thought to the
> obedience of Christ.

This is exactly what happened in Poland in that
Communist Youth Club. *Through praise and worship,
we launched our spiritual weapons, "pulling down
strongholds." That was the key, the connection.* Another Scripture reinforcing this concept came to mind,
Ephesians 6:12: "For we wrestle not against flesh and
blood, but against principalities, against powers,
against the rulers of the darkness of this world, against
spiritual wickedness in high places."

This verse, Ephesians 6:12, with 2 Corinthians 10:4, served as a special key to intriguing insights as to the extent and nature of our warfare against spiritual strongholds.

The Greek word *epouranios* is used five times in Ephesians: Eph. 1:3; Eph. 1:20; Eph. 2:6; Eph. 3:10; and, Eph. 6:12. In the first four instances, it is translated in the *King James Version* as "heavenly places." In the last instance, for some reason, it is translated "high places," although it is the same word. Understanding this makes it very clear that our spiritual warfare takes place in "heavenly places," or, in heaven.

This was a disturbing concept to me, for it implied that Satan was loose in the "heavenlies," and I'd always believed that Satan resided in hell. But then, my continued study revealed that there actually were three "heavenlies," or, heavens.

In 2 Corinthians 12:2 Paul writes about an experience where he, or someone he knew, was ". . . caught up to the third heaven," which he then describes as being paradise, where God dwells. *If there is a third heaven, logic dictates that there must also be a first and second heaven.*

The first heaven, I believe, is descibed in Psalms 19:1: "The heavens declare the glory of God; and the firmament sheweth his handywork." The second heaven I found described in Revelation 14:6: "And I saw another angel fly in the midst of heaven, having the everlasting gospel to preach unto them that dwell on the earth, and to every nation, and kindred, and tongue, and people." In the Greek, the word for "midst" is a single compound noun, and the phrase could better be translated as "the mid-heaven," or, "the middle heaven."

When Satan was cast out of the presence of God along with one-third of the angels, I believe he established his "command post" in the second, or middle, heaven. That Satan is in the heavenlies now is made clear in Revelation 12:7-8: "And there was war in heaven: Michael and his angels fought against the dragon; and the dragon fought and his angels, And prevailed not; neither was their place found any more in heaven."

This description of the end-times warfare that takes place in the future makes it clear that Satan and his fallen angels occupy a heaven. It is here, in his heavenly realm that Satan has organized his "principalities . . . powers . . . rulers of the darkness of this world . . . spiritual wickedness in [the heavenlies]."

These are the strongholds described in 2 Corinthians 10:4. And these are the strongholds that we will pull down with our *mighty* weapons of warfare.

This excites me! God wants His Church, His people, moving into areas of spiritual warfare in a much more involved manner than we have yet realized. In the end-times, the Church, with Michael and God's angels, will cast Satan out of his heaven, and will do so through the power of the Blood of Christ: "And they overcame him by the blood of the Lamb, and by the word of their testimony . . . (Rev. 12:11a)."

This indicates to me that we have been living far beneath the authority and power that God has allocated to His Church, since we have available to us *right now* the same power of Jesus' Name, His Word, and His Blood.

It is time for believers to gain a proper understanding of their authority, and the full extent of the spiritual warfare raging around them. It is time to more effectively and victoriously enter the battle, and begin pull-ing down the enemy's strongholds. Healing and deliverance — the pulling down of strongholds — will come through praise and worship!

3

Spiritual Strongholds

There are essentially three areas in which spiritual strongholds are operative: individuals' thoughts; thought-systems (ideologies, philosophies, etc.); and, in geographical and political areas.

Personal strongholds: our own thoughts

When the Lord impressed upon me the words of 2 Corinthians 10:4, immediately, I saw that strongholds were the major stumbling blocks of God's people. It was not difficult for me to believe that strongholds could include physical disease, spiritual oppression, temptation, financial bondage, relational difficulties in marriage and family.

However, I knew there was more to the subject of strongholds than what I had uncovered thus far. In further meditation on the text, my focus turned to verse 5, "Casting down imaginations and every high thing that exalts itself against the knowledge of God and bringing into captivity every thought to the obedience of Christ."

It suddenly occurred to me that the strongholds that Paul talked about in verse 4 were further described in verse 5. Evil imaginations could be strongholds. Every high or proud thing that exalts itself against God could be a stronghold. Then Paul says we are to bring into captivity every thought to the obedience of Christ. Suddenly I saw something that had never occurred to me before. *Paul was describing thoughts as strongholds.* This opened a brand new area of spiritual revelation to me.

I immediately began a study of thoughts in scripture. It became patently clear Satan's modus operandi was to control by the power of suggestive thoughts. A quick examination of the word underscored this observation.

In Acts chapter 8, when Peter and John had come to Samaria to minister, Simon the sorcerer tried to buy the gift of the Holy Spirit from Peter. Peter said to Simon, "Pray that the thought of thine heart might be forgiven thee." Simon obviously was motivated by a thought. Where did that thought come from? It came from the enemy. Peter said in effect, "Satan has put a thought in your heart. You have accepted it as your own and acted upon it. Now you pray for God to forgive you for that thought."

The Bible says concerning the betrayal of Jesus, "Now Satan, having put in the heart of Judas to betray Him." Satan dropped a thought into the mind and heart of Judas. Judas bought that thought and it destroyed him. Matthew 15:18,19 says, "But those things which proceed out of the mouth come forth from the heart; and they defile the man. For out of the heart proceed evil thoughts...." Then it names the thoughts: murders, adulteries, fornication, thefts, false witness, blasphemy, etc.

Suddenly it became clear. Satan has been operating in my life by establishing a stronghold based on a thought system. In Matthew, Chapter 13, Jesus teaches the disciples the parable of the sower. In the parable, the sower sows seeds on four different kinds of ground. Some seeds fell by the wayside and the fowls or birds came and picked them up. In verse 19 of the same chapter, Jesus interprets what that verse meant.

He said, "when anyone heareth the word of the kingdom and understands it not, then cometh the wicked one and catches away that which was sown in his heart." We have here an incredible description of the power of the enemy. He obviously has the ability to read our thoughts. When the seed of the gospel is sown in our heart, he can catch that seed away by sowing something else in our mind.

There is no doubt in my mind that the modus operandi of Satan's kingdom is to create strongholds in our lives by the manipulation of our thought life.

David knew what he was talking about when he said, "I will set no wicked thing before mine eyes" (Ps. 101:3); he knew the secret of guarding his mind. He also said, "Let the words of my mouth and the meditation of my heart, be acceptable in thy sight, Oh Lord" (Ps. 19:14). The meditations of our heart, our thought life, should be acceptable to God.

The area of our thoughts is both the first and final battlefield. The warfare is in the mind before it goes to other areas. It's amazing in a practical sense to see how the Devil works against us on a day-by-day basis.

One of the tools of the Devil is to make you believe that God is waiting to pounce on you the moment you step out of line. These thoughts are not coming from God, but from the Devil. One of the tricks of the Devil is to make us think that these thoughts are actually the convicting of the Holy Spirit. This is one of his clever means of confusing believers and turning them in the wrong direction.

A lying thought can become a stronghold. These thoughts can create tormenting fear inside of us; fear directly from Satan himself. If we accept the thoughts and live in the torment they produce, we become bound.

A friend wrote of a vision he experienced. The Lord spoke to him and said, "I will show you how evil spirits get hold of people as they are allowed to." In the vision he saw a woman he immediately recognized as being the former wife of a minister he knew.

The Lord said, "This woman was a child of mine. She was in the ministry with her husband. One day an evil spirit came to her and whispered in her ear, 'You are a beautiful woman. You could have fame, popularity, and wealth. But you have been cheated in life by your Christian walk.' The woman recognized this as an evil spirit, and said, 'Get thee behind me Satan,' and the spirit left her for a period. But it came back. He whispered again, 'You are a beautiful woman, but you have been robbed by your Christianity.' Again, she said, 'Satan I resist you in the the name of Jesus.'

He left, then returned. He whispered the same thing. This time she began to entertain those thoughts. She liked to think she was beautiful. As she began to think along these lines, she became obsessed with the Devil's thoughts."

Then in the vision my friend saw the woman become as transparent as glass, and he saw in her mind a black dot. That dot represented the thought planted in her mind by the enemy.

The Lord said, "At first she was oppressed on the outside, but as she allowed the Devil's suggestion to take hold of her thoughts, her mind became obsessed. She could have resisted. She could have refused to think those thoughts, and the spirit would have fled from her. But she chose otherwise. Finally, she left her husband, went out into the world seeking the fame and wealth which the Devil offered. She became involved with one man after another. After a time the thought possessed her spirit."

In the vision my friend saw the black dot move from her head to her heart, and then the woman said, "I don't want the Lord anymore, just leave me alone." One mighty lie from the Devil placed into your mind can hold you in a place of sickness, suffering, and torment.

Over the years I have seen Christians endure violent attacks in their mind and body. I have seen some suffer untold agony for years merely because of a thought. The Devil tells them that their loving, heavenly Father sent the sickness. He tells them they must suffer patiently and be faithful for this is God's doing — a lie from hell! Wrong thought has destroyed the lives of so many people. God doesn't do that to His children.

Corporate strongholds: thought-systems

While each of us wrestle with strongholds of thought on a personal level, we also are influenced by corporate thought-systems: political ideologies, philosophies and world religious beliefs. Communism and secular humanism are examples of these corporate thought-systems.

Easy access to print and other media have allowed these thought-systems to spread throughout the world, and they have permeated many societies with their destructive lies. I call these thought-systems "thought-bombs" because they actually are weapons being used in spiritual warfare. And when they impact on a society, they literally "blow-up," wreaking spiritual havoc and destruction.

Communism is more than an ideology; it is a tremendously powerful stronghold—a spiritually based "thought-bomb" generated by Satan—that holds control over the minds and lives of a vast number of people. I realized long ago that if I was going to be effective ministering in the Communist world, I must take authority over these strongholds, and pull them down with prayer and fasting.

It is crucial for us to be aware of these "thought-bombs" that are influencing us and our children, especially through our educational systems and media. One of the great strategies of Satan has been to radically condition the thinking of mankind through the deceptive teaching and philosophy of the world's great thinkers.

Used by the Deceiver: the men behind the ideas

Immanuel Kant was a German philosopher who lived in Prussia from 1724 to 1804. His "thought-bombs" still have a great impact on the civilized world. Prior to Kant, man thought in terms of cause-and-effect. Values were absolute; you did not have to experience to know, or, see to believe. Kant introduced the "thought-bomb" that knowledge was based purely on experience; if you could not see, hear, touch, taste, or smell it, you could not believe in it. Thus, there were no absolutes in the area of personal belief. Kant's ideas laid the foundation for philosophies that followed.

George Wilhelm Friedrich Hegel took the ideas of Kant and developed a philosophy that became the foundation for the ideas of Karl Marx and Adolf Hitler. According to Hegelian thought, everything is relevant. Again, there are no absolutes since we cannot reason from cause to effect. We must think solely in terms of subjectivity.

This existentialism has been so powerful that even the average college student today doesn't really believe in the possibility of absolute truth. Relevant, existential thinking is now evident in the earliest levels of our elementary educational process. It is a "thought-bomb" that has America by the throat and many Christians aren't even aware of it.

Karl Marx developed his philosophy from Hegel's. According to Marx, property owners are exploiters, and workers are the exploited. Marx applied the art of split-reasoning, or dialectics, to this inevitable class struggle that was supposed to remake the world into a classless society. Marxism is a complete thought-system which permeates education, religion, trade, economics, culture, and so forth. It espouses that the end justifies the means. Marx's goals were simple: collectivize, centralize, and then control.

In my many years of contact with the Communist world, I have come to realize that Communism is not just a political ideology, it is a religion; a religion that promises a false utopia to its followers. The state is worshipped in the place of God.

Charles Darwin introduced a thought-system that still molds our educational systems. He stated that all forms of life, including man, evolved from lower animal forms: man is merely an animal. In contrast to the Genesis account of creation, Darwin took the Hegelian and Marxist concept of *thesis, antithesis, and synthesis,* and applied it to the scientific method. He promoted the idea of "survival of the fittest" for humans, as well as animals. The theory of evolution, followed to its logical conclusion, has caused many to fall into a life of immorality and despair.

Sigmund Freud was very attracted to Darwin's theory. As the father of psychoanalysis, his ideas have shaped the mental attitudes of this century. Freud professed that humans were motivated simply by pleasure, everything starting and ending with sex. He believed that man is repressed by a society which hinders the fulfillment of his drive to gratify his erotic desires. Freud's ideas, too, are based on the belief that there is no purpose in man's existence, that "everything goes." He laid the foundation for permissiveness that is shaking our society today.

Vladimir Lenin was the builder of modern Communism. He referred to religion as the opiate of the people. He used terror, murder, and secret police to crush opposition to his ideas, and emerged as the dictator of Soviet Russia. In 1917 Lenin declared, "We will destroy everything, and on the ruins we will build our temple. It will be a temple for the happiness of all, but we will destroy the entire bourgeoisie; grind it to a powder. I will be merciless with all counter-revolutionaries." Communism essentially is an extension of the concept of "survival of the fittest."

The time has come for us to be aware of these very powerful "thought-bombs" that influence us and permeate our society. We must realize that the power of praise and worship in a believer's life can have great power in overcoming these evil strongholds in the lives of other people. I have seen it happen countless times. I have seen the power of praise and worship turned against the "thought-bombs" that dominate the thinking of other people, and they have become open and susceptible to the message of the Word of God.

Geographical and political strongholds

In Daniel 9 and 10, we are given a clear example of

how strongholds operate over geographical areas. It is important to keep in mind that spiritual warfare takes place in the heavenlies, but the effects of that warfare are seen upon the earth and upon people.

Daniel, after reading the prophecies of Jeremiah "understood . . . that [the Lord] would accomplish seventy years in the desolations of Jerusalem" (Dan. 9:1). As Daniel studied this prophecy, he realized that the 70 years had passed, and according to the Lord's calendar, it was time for deliverance. Daniel also understood the importance and power of prayer in receiving God's promises, and so he "set [his] face unto the Lord God, to seek by prayer and supplications, with fasting, and sackcloth, and ashes" (Dan. 9:3).

For three weeks, Daniel sought forgiveness from the Lord for himself and for Israel. Finally, on the twenty-first day of his fast an angel came to Daniel and said, ". . . Fear not, Daniel: for from the first day that thou didst set thine heart to understand, and to chasten thyself before thy God, thy words were heard, and I am come for thy words. But the prince of the kingdom of Persia withstood me one and twenty days: but, lo, Michael, one of the chief princes, came to help me; and I remained there with the kings of Persia" (Dan. 10:12, 13).

It is clear to me that this confrontation took place in the second heaven. This prince of Persia undoubtedly is one of the same princes that Paul speaks about in Ephesians 6:12. He obviously had great power and authority and was able to withstand God's messenger, making it impossible for him to get through to Daniel. However, God dispatched Michael to the messenger's aid.

A quick study of Michael in Scripture reveals that he was the chief of the warrior angels. In fact, he was the archangel in charge of the nation of Israel. Daniel 10:21 indicates that Michael was the prince of Israel. Because he was a warrior angel, it was no problem for Michael to deal with the evil prince of Persia and to release the messenger so he could reach Daniel.

It is interesting to note that Persia was the ruling nation in Daniel's day. The next great world-power that would overcome and destroy Persia was the kingdom of Greece under Alexander the Great. These countries had princes in the spiritual areas that were influencing their geographical and political destinies (see Dan. 10:20).

Spiritual warfare dealing with strongholds is astounding in its implications. Satan has delegated evil princes to be in charge of countries and geographical areas. I suspect that when the Americans were being held hostage in the embassy in Teheran several years ago, we were not dealing with the Ayatollah or the Iranian people. We were dealing literally with the prince of Persia; the ancient nation of Persia now being divided into Iran and Afghanistan. That prince is still actively doing everything he can to control the destiny of his country.

A modern illustration revealing the influence of strongholds in geographical areas comes from a story that appeared in a magazine called "Acts" published by the World Map organization.

A missionary was working in a new area in the mountains of Brazil and Uruguay in South America. He was witnessing in a village situated directly on the border of the two nations. In fact, the border ran down the center of main street. He was distributing Gospel tracts during a shopping day when he noticed something quite unusual.

On the Uruguayan side of the main street, no one would accept his Gospel tracts. But, on the Brazilian side, everyone accepted the tracts graciously, and were open to hearing his testimony concerning his faith in Christ. He moved back and forth across the street with the same bewildering results. Then he noticed a woman who had refused his tract on the Uruguayan side of the street cross to the Brazilian side. He followed her and again offered her a tract. She accepted it gratefully, and he was able to witness to her about the Lord.

The missionary realized something very strange was going on. He began checking with other missionaries and believers in that particular area of Brazil. He discovered there was a group of Christians who had entered into spiritual warfare. They were involved in intercessory prayer, and had literally taken authority over and bound the prince in that area of Brazil.

Wherever the Gospel was preached there, tremendous revival was occurring. But the awesome realization that shook the missionary was the fact that the revival ended at the geographical boundary; the stronghold over that area of Brazil ended at the border in the center of main street.

Jesus described this type of a situation involving the binding of strongholds. In Matthew 12, Jesus replies to the Pharisee's accusation that He is casting out demons with the authority of Beelzebub:

25 . . . Every kingdom divided against itself is brought to desolation; and every city or house divided against itself shall not stand:
26 And if Satan cast out Satan, he is divided against himself; how shall then his kingdom stand?
29 Or else how can one enter into a strong man's house, and spoil his goods, except he first bind the strong man? and then he will spoil his house.

The Christians in Brazil had bound the strong man by prayer and fasting, and then they were able to spoil his house in terms of spiritual warfare. The same thing happened when Daniel prayed. Daniel's prayers brought additional "firepower" into the spiritual warfare, and thus the strong man, the prince of Persia, was held at bay so God's messenger could get through.

The Brazilian Christians and Daniel, using the power of their weapons, entered into spiritual warfare, and literally pulled down strongholds.

Daniel was successful in influencing the history of an entire nation through his fasting and prayer. Angels began to move in heavenly realms in response to the prayer of a group of Christians here on the earth. This gives us only an inkling of the powerful influence that we can exert in the area of spiritual strongholds. If we can pull down strongholds with our spiritual weapons, then a great spiritual victory for the church can be ours.

The time has come for us to begin to move into the principles of God's Word and begin to let our spiritual warfare be manifested in the heavenly realm.

We do not wrestle with flesh and blood, but we wrestle with principalities, powers, and strongholds in the heavenlies. When we move against them, we will see physical manifestations here on the earth. We will see people healed. We will see people delivered. We will see people set free from all kinds of bondage. We will see homes healed. We will see tremendous manifestations of healing in marriage, and in every other area where people are bound.

This is the manifestation of miracles in the area of strongholds. This was one insight I gained from the Holy Spirit as I tried to relate praise and worship to the area of healing and deliverance.

Satan's sinister strategy

The Christian who fails to take up his weapons against the Devil is already defeated. There can be no victory in the Christian life without a fight. We have to know the Devil's strategy before we are able to counteract it. One important consideration concerning the Devil's access to our minds is how he exercises control over the mind. Is he actually able to put his thoughts in our minds? Can he interfere with our ability to choose our thoughts?

Although there are cases of demon *oppression* where the enemy has been allowed the power to control someone's thoughts, on the whole he does not have the right to violate our free will. Even our faith is based on our ability to choose, to respond to divine revelation. The Devil does not influence us by forcing his thoughts on us. In that sense we would be able to say, "The Devil made me do it," and not accept responsibility. He wants us judged for *our* wickedness and *our* sin, therefore *he operates in the area of suggestion.* We either reject, or accept his suggestions.

He knows us better than we know ourselves. We very quickly pass over the weak areas of our life and the mistakes of the past. We want to forget them as quickly as we can, and we should.

But all of these things are stored in our subconscious mind, and he is an expert at triggering our worst memories. At the right moment he is able to trigger a thought that opens us to a sin of the flesh. This is where his awesome power lies. He has a complete understanding of human frailty and this gives him the ability to present the most appetizing suggestions to us at precisely the right time.

He often will appeal to the natural mind in such a

way that the mind doesn't even know that it is doing something wrong. His lies are so presentable that we accept them as truth. Most Christians don't suspect the real source of much of their thought. They think because it came out of their mind they must accept responsibility for it. *When we accept the thought, we actually buy responsibility for the thought, and become guilty for the thought.* The thoughts come through our minds but we don't have to act upon them and make them our own.

This is what Paul means in 2 Corinthians 10:5 by, "casting down imaginations" and "bringing every thought into captivity." We must have a strategy designed to stop the power of the thoughts, to pull down the strongholds of the mind. Our strategy, our defensive firepower, is praise and worship.

Growing God's thoughts

Praise is the taking of God's thoughts and superimposing them over the thoughts from the enemy. Praise, as it relates to our great spiritual weapons, the Word, the Name and the Blood, enlists the power of God to change and transform the thinking of the mind. This is just part of the power that Paul is talking about in 2 Corinthians 10:4. It is so important that through praise we learn the discipline of using our spiritual weapons.

This is why the Psalms are being sung as choruses in many of our churches. There is power in singing the Word of God. When you take the thoughts of God, and enter into praise, and uplift the name of God, you are literally tearing down the strongholds of the Devil.

Thoughts are like seeds. When you plant seeds they will bring forth after their kind. When you plant an acorn, it will bring forth an oak tree. When you plant a carrot seed, it will bring forth a carrot. Our thoughts are like seeds and they create after their kind. If we focus our thoughts on poverty, it doesn't matter how much wealth a rich uncle may give us, sooner or later we'll be living in poverty. Thoughts create the situation around us. You can determine the situation in which you live by the seed thoughts that you send forth around you.

"For as he thinketh in his heart, so is he" (Pr. 23:7), the Word of God says. That is why the Word of God is so important in transforming our thoughts.

The Bible is filled with the thoughts of God. We are called to replace every thought the Devil gives us with one of God's thoughts. When the Devil says you're not saved, answer him with John 1:12: "But as many as received him [Christ], to them gave he power to become the sons of God, even to them that believe on his name." That thought becomes a weapon, a powerful tool for pulling down the stronghold of the Devil.

Learn to put that verse into a song. Make a chorus out of it, especially if the Devil has been trying to rob you of your joy of salvation. *Let praise and worship link up with the power of His Word.* Learn to focus it against the bondage of the Devil.

Learn a verse that answers every temptation that the Devil brings. If he tells you you're going to die early in life, quote Psalm 91:16: "With long life will I satsify him, and shew him my salvation." If the Devil says you're not going to get well, tell him, ". . . with his stripes we are healed (Isa. 53:5)." If the Devil tells you God has made you sick, quote Psalm 103:2, 3: "Bless the Lord, O my soul, and forget not all his benefits: Who forgiveth all thine iniquities; who healeth all thy diseases."

When we do this, we are following the same strategy that Jesus used in the wilderness. When the Devil came to Him with the three temptations, Jesus replied to each with the words, "It is written." Jesus went to the Source of his strength and power which was the Word of God, and the lesser power of the Devil's temptation was overcome by the greater power of the Word.

Praise and worship enters into the equation when we take the word and make it an act of praise unto God, and begin to bless God through the exercise of praise. The more we praise God for the power of the thought of God's Word, the more the strongholds that bind us will be torn down, and we will obtain deliverance and healing in every area of our lives.

4

Spiritual Weapons: The Word

For the weapons of our warfare are mighty through God to the pulling down of strongholds. What are the believer's weapons?

Strongholds exercise a tremendous power in our lives. If we focus our spiritual eyes on strongholds, we easily can be overcome by the power they exert. Thank God, His Word gives us great hope.

God has given us weapons that work. In Ephesians 6, Paul outlines the defensive weaponry of the believer. He speaks about the shoes of the preparation of the Gospel of peace; the girdle of truth; the helmet of salvation; the shield of faith; the breastplate of righteousness. However, one weapon in this list is not defensive, and that is the Word of God.

In 2 Corinthians 10, Paul says, "Our weapons are mighty to pull down strongholds." What weapons is he referring to? Obviously from the context of the verse, he is talking about *offensive* weaponry. Every believer at one time or another in his life has to ask himself, "What do I have to fight with? What weapons has God given me that will be effective in pulling down the strongholds of the Devil in my life?"

There are three primary weapons God has given to

every believer. They have an intrinsic power in them
that is generated by the Holy Spirit. The three weapons
are: the Word of God; the Name of Jesus; and, the Blood
of Jesus.

There is an explosive power in the Word to cast
down strongholds. The Name of Jesus has innate
power in the mouth of the believer. In Revelation 12:11,
it says, "And they overcame him [the Devil] by the
blood of the Lamb, and by the word of their testimony." They went on the offensive against the Devil
with the power of the Blood.

In the following three chapters, I will explain the
three weapons that God has given to believers. In this
chapter, we will deal with the Word of God. The Scripture outlines the working of the Word of God. *The Bible*
reveals how to make the Word work for us. How to attack strongholds with the Word of God.

The power of the Word

The Bible declares itself to be the Word of God.
However, there also are many portions of Scripture that
refer to Jesus Christ as the Word of God. John 1:1 says,
"In the beginning was the Word, and the Word was
with God, and the Word was God." Christ is the *living*
Word of God; the Scripture is the written Word of God.

It is absolutely impossible to overemphasize the
power of God's Word in the life of the believer. John
14:23 says, "If a man love me, he will keep my words:
and my Father will love him, and we will come unto
him, and make our abode with him." Our attitude toward God must be the same toward His Word. We can
never say that we love God more than we love His
Word. If you want to know how much God means in
your life, then examine the place you've given His
Word in your life. *God means as much to you as His*

Word means to you; just that and no more.

But the Scripture claims power for itself. In John 6:63, Jesus said, ". . . the words that I speak unto you, they are spirit, and they are life." In 1 Thessalonians 2:13, Paul says, "For this cause also thank we God without ceasing, because, when ye received the word of God which ye heard of us, ye received it not as the word of men, but as it is in truth, the word of God, which effectually worketh also in you that believe."

There is a working of the Word of God. There is an innate spiritual energy. There is a power from God that makes the Word a weapon that you and I are to use. There is life in God's Word. There is spirit. It is active. It is more powerful than a two-edged sword.

The Word gives faith

There are several effects that the Word of God produces in the Believer. The first is faith. Romans 10:17 says, "So then faith cometh by hearing, and hearing by the word of God." How does faith come? It comes by hearing. How do we hear? By the Word of God. There are three successive stages in the development of faith in the life of the believer. First, God's Word is proclaimed; second, the believer hears; third, faith develops out of hearing.

Hearing is more than just listening. It is an attitude of aroused interest and attention, a hunger to receive and to grasp the power of the message as it is spoken. Faith develops out of that hearing, but a hearing that is more than just listening to a Sunday morning sermon. If faith is to develop, we must devote a considerable amount of time to hearing God's Word over and over again.

The Word gives health

God's Word provides physical health and strength

for the body. In Psalms 107:20, the Bible says, "[God] sent His word, and healed them, and delivered them . . ." In Isaiah 55:11, God says, "[My Word] shall not return unto me void, but it shall accomplish that which I please, and it shall prosper in the thing whereto I sent it." God absolutely guarantees to provide healing through His Word. *If He has sent His Word to heal, then His Word is going to heal.*

Proverbs 4:20 through 22 has a great message in this regard:

20 My son, attend to my words; incline thine ear unto my sayings.
21 Let them not depart from thine eyes; keep them in the midst of thine heart.
22 For they are life unto those that find them, and health [or medicine] to all their flesh.

These verses express plainly the power of the Word of God to heal. When we attend to His Word, when we incline our ear to hear the Word of God, when we keep His Word ever before our eyes, when we meditate on His Word, then the Word of God becomes life and provides health to our flesh. When the Syrophenician woman came to Jesus asking for healing for her daughter, Jesus said, "It is not right to take the children's bread and to cast it to dogs."

Jesus equated healing with bread. Bread is a basic of our diet, something that we eat daily. Healing is spiritual bread. That healing flows to us through the Word of God. There is life in the Word of God to bring physical healing to our human flesh.

The Word gives new birth

God's Word gives us new birth, or the born-again experience. In 1 Peter 1:23, it says, "Being born again, not of corruptible seed, but of incorruptible, by the word of God, which liveth and abideth forever." This verse declares clearly we are born-again by the power and working of the incorruptible Word of God. Peter here likens the Word of God to a seed. The seed is the divine, incorruptible, eternal Word of God. When you sow a seed in the ground, life is resident in the seed, and that life will express itself in a plant that grows forth from the seed.

The same is true of the Word of God. When it is sown in the heart of the believer, it grows and brings life to the believer. This is the great working of the Word of God in every life. The true Christian who has been born-again by the incorruptible seed of God's Word has within himself the ability to lead a life of victory over sin. He has within him the seed of the nature of God. He has been born into the kingdom of God by the power of the Word of God which "liveth and abideth forever."

The Word gives light

God's Word brings light and revelation to the believer. Psalm 119:130 states, "The entrance of thy words giveth light; it giveth understanding unto the simple." When God's Word enters our heart, it brings light and understanding with it. James 1:22 through 23 describes the Word of God as a mirror that brings spiritual revelation.

When the believer beholds himself and looks into the mirror of the Word, he recognizes the kind of person he is before God. The Word of God as a mirror reveals positive and negative. When we look in the mirror, the Word will reveal spiritual uncleaness and sickness of any kind. As we respond, we can find immediate forgiveness, cleansing, and healing.

The mirror of God's Word also reveals what God sees when He looks at us. It shows us our robe of righteousness and our garment of salvation. It shows us to be truly children of God, joint heirs of Jesus Christ. We begin to realize "If any man be in Christ, he is a new creature, a new creation." The mirror of God's Word shows us all these things.

The Word gives food

God's Word provides food for the believer at every level of spiritual development. 1 Peter 2:1, 2 declares, "Wherefore laying aside all malice, and all guile, and hypocrisies, and envies, and all evil speakings, As newborn babes, desire the sincere milk of the word, that ye may grow thereby." Spiritual babes will find nourishment in God's Word. It will be the sincere milk of His own Word.

In Matthew 4:4, Jesus says, "It is written, Man shall not live by bread alone, but by every word that proceedeth out of the mouth of God." Jesus here indicates that God's Word is like bread in the believer's diet, a staple. It must be eaten all the time. There is spiritual nourishment in the Word of God. In Hebrews 5:12 through 14, the writer relates the Word of God to strong meat. It is spiritual food for every level of the believer's life; milk, bread, and strong meat.

The Word gives cleansing

God's Word cleanses the believer's life. John 15:3 states, "Now ye are clean through the word which I have spoken unto you." The Word has a cleansing operation in the life of the believer. In Ephesians 5:25, 26, it says, ". . . Christ also loved the church, and gave himself for it; That he might sanctify and cleanse it with the washing of water by the word." The operation of God's Word here is compared to the washing of pure water. God's Word will remind us of our sin.

As we listen, and live the Word, there is an inward cleansing that is exercised in our life by the power of God's Word. The Word of God contains all that we shall ever need for life and godliness as 2 Peter 1:4 declares. We can escape the corruption of the world and be made partakers of the divine nature through the promises of God.

The Word gives victory

God's Word brings victory to the life of the believer. In Ephesians 6:17, the Word of God is called the sword of the spirit. In other words, the Word of God is our sword from the Holy Spirit for our fight in spiritual warfare. David declared in Psalm 119:11, "Thy word have I hid in mine heart, that I might not sin against thee." There is power in the Word that makes us victorious over the temptations of the Devil.

The Devil will do all he can to keep a believer ignorant of the power of God's Word. Satan knows once a believer becomes aware of the power of God's Word on his lips that he will begin to stand against Satan's strongholds. The Devil fears this more than anything else.

It is interesting to see how Jesus used the Word of God against the Devil in the wilderness. Satan came to Christ with three temptations. Christ answered Satan with three quotations from Scripture. The Word was His sword and He used it to overcome the Devil.

It also is interesting to note in Luke 4:1, that when Jesus went into the wilderness, he was *full of* the Holy Spirit, but in Luke 4:14, it says Jesus "returned *in the power of* the Spirit." There is an obvious difference between *being filled with* the Spirit and *moving in the power of* the Spirit. *This difference of Spiritual maturity is the difference between having the potential of the Spirit's power, and actually using the power of the Word of God to defeat Satan.* This is spiritual warfare.

By learning the power of the Word to overcome the Devil, and using the Word of God as a great weapon, we move into an area of faith where the power of the Holy Spirit begins to move in our lives. There is no more powerful weapon than the Word of God. We must be thoroughly equipped in the Word of God with a knowledge and understanding of its total authority.

John says in 1 John 2:14, "I have written unto you, young men, because ye are strong, and the word of God abideth in you, and ye have overcome the wicked one." Many of us don't understand the importance of the Word in our lives. It is the weapon of the Word that will make us stand. It is the weapon of the Word that gives us victory. It is the weapon of the Word that makes Satan flee.

Rhema and logos: A word study

From the Word comes faith, healing, new birth, spiritual nourishment, revelation, cleansing, and victory over Satan. What great power there is in our weapon, but it is important that we understand the difference between *rhema* and *logos.*

In the original Greek of the New Testament, there are two Greek words translated as "word." One is *logos,* and the other is *rhema.* They each have a distinct meaning. *Logos* refers to the unchanging self-existent Word of God. David says in Psalms 119:89, "For ever, O Lord, thy word [logos] is settled in heaven." *Logos* refers to the entire written Word of God. It is the complete revelation of God in Scripture.

Rhema is derived from the verb "to speak." In Romans 10:17, Paul says, "So then faith cometh by hearing, and hearing by the word of God." The word in that verse is *rhema*. Faith comes by hearing the *rhema* of God. *Rhema* is a word God speaks especially to us, relating directly to a problem or challenge we are facing. *Logos* is the entire council of God. It is vast, it is constant. *Rhema* takes a portion of the *logos* and applies it directly to something in our experience. It is for a particular time in our lives.

Our response to God's spoken word must be to hear. How can we hear the Word of God? Proverbs 4:20 through 22 tells us how we can hear the Word of the Lord. First, we must attend to the Word; second, incline our ear; third, let it not depart from our eyes; fourth, meditate on it, or keep it in the midst of our heart.

If we will give our undivided attention to what God is saying; if we will bow our knees to the Word and listen attentively; if we will take our eyes off all other things and focus only on what God's Word says to us; if we will continue to hide God's Word in our heart and meditate upon it so that it begins to penetrate every area of our being — *this is how we hear God's Word.*

Notice the relationship of *rhema* to speaking. It always has something to do with the mouth, or voice. In Matthew 4:4, when Jesus is answering the Devil in the wilderness, he says, "Man shall not live by bread alone, but by every word [rhema] that proceedeth out of the mouth of God." This is an amazing statement when you examine it. Jesus said we are not to live on bread alone, we are not to be concerned only with the physical. But, our spiritual bread is every *rhema* that is spoken from the mouth of God.

The word "proceedeth" is in the present tense in the Greek, indicating there is a word proceeding out of the mouth of God toward you and me *right now*. This word is our daily bread. This word is for us, right now. We are asked to hear it. We are asked to pick up the *rhema* as it comes. As we are willing to hear God's Word, that *rhema* produces faith in our hearts and we move in the power of faith to see miracles.

Living the *rhema*

God speaks a *rhema* to our hearts by the power of the Holy Spirit. As we meditate on that word and faith springs up within, then we are to express our faith by the word of our mouth. As our words give expression to our faith, the Word of God in our mouth goes forth with the power of God Himself.

This is how the Word becomes our weapon. This is what Paul refers to in 2 Corinthians 10:4, "the weapons of our warfare are mighty." It is this *rhema* word of God spoken to us, converted into faith, and transformed out of our mouths, that brings the power of God against the temptation and strongholds of the Devil.

Remember the words of Paul in 1 Thessalonians 2:13: "For this cause also thank we God without ceasing, because, when ye received the word of God which ye heard of us, ye received it not as the word of men, but as it is in truth, the word of God, which effectually worketh also in you that believe." The Word will have great power for you, but only as you make it work.

You can be a hearer of the Word all of your life, but never do it. It is only when we *talk* the Word of God, determine to make it work by the power of the words of our mouth, speaking the Word of God into existence, *then* we begin to see the miracles inherent in the Word itself.

Resisting Satan

The Devil does not flee from the presence of the Word of God in our minds. He doesn't flee from us just because we happen to read the Bible. He flees only when we *resist*. How do we resist? The same way Jesus resisted. He said, "Get thee hence, Satan, *for it is written* . . ." Jesus used the Word of God against the Devil. *There must come a time when we make a deliberate choice to use the Word of God against the stronghold of the Devil.* It does not happen automatically. We must do the resisting.

Just because there is a motor in my car doesn't mean the car is going to go anywhere. I must activate the power in that motor by turning on the key. We have within us the great power of our almighty God. There is a spiritual motor inside every believer, but we must turn on the key. We must resist, speaking the Word of God. The Word of God spoken from our lips will make the Devil flee. It will tear down strongholds.

Psalms 119:130 says, "The entrance of thy word giveth light." When we speak God's Word with our lips, the light of God will shine in the midst of darkness. When we take God's Word and turn it on the Devil, declaring in Jesus' name that God's Word is greater than any stronghold, the stronghold will yield.

When the Devil says you are no good, remind him of 2 Corinthians 5:17: "Therefore if any man be in Christ he is a new creature, old things are passed away, behold all things have become new."

When the Devil says you are not saved, point to 1 John 5:11, 12a, "And this is the record, that God has given to us eternal life, and this life is in his Son. He that has the son hath life."

When the Devil says worry, remind him God says "don't worry about anything." When he says, be sick, remind him of God's Word, "By His stripes, I am healed." When he says be afraid, remind him of Jesus' words, "My peace, I give unto you." When the Devil says you are defeated, remind him that, "we are more than conquerors through Him that loves us."

It is one of the great learning experiences of the believer's life to see how quickly Satan flees when God's Word is fired at him. The results depend on how seriously you take God's Word and how willing you are to stand in faith and speak to him. He knows if you believe what you are saying.

It is vital to develop a plan for resisting the Devil. He will attack us in our areas of weakness. I have them, you have them. We can know where Satan will concentrate his attack, and prepare for him beforehand.

Galatians 5:19 through 21 gives us a list of men's weaknesses: lust, idolatry, laziness, touchiness, judgementalism, factiousness, gossip, worry, pessimism, selfishness, distraction, lying, dissatisfaction, easily discouraged, wastefulness, abusiveness, covetousness, depression, fears, procrastination. An examination of this list may make you aware of areas in your life where Satan will attack you. Find a scripture for that weakness. Scripture speaks strength to us, and is an answer to the stronghold of the Devil.

Every time the enemy attacks, we can bring God's Word against him. We call out his name and say, "Get thee hence, Satan! Get out of here, Devil! *For it is written* . . ." He won't go away until you tell him to.

One thing the devil is terrified of is the Name of Jesus. It brings back to him the awful memory of Calvary. It reminds him of what happened on the cross. He remembers that he was openly defeated by the work of Jesus Christ. He remembers that he made a terrible mistake in crucifying the Savior. The Name of Jesus makes him shudder. It is a shock to his system.

When we stand in the "power of attorney" in Jesus' Name with the Word of God on our lips, Satan's defeat is certain. But we must speak against Satan in the power of the Name. When we speak the Word of God in the power of Jesus' Name, the Holy Spirit explodes it against the strongholds that bind us. We attack the Devil's thoughts, and they lose their ability to hold our mind.

Praising with the Word

When we determine to praise the Lord in the midst of satanic attack, we are operating on the basis of Scriptural principle. When we praise the Lord in the midst of family problems, financial problems, sickness, fear, and discouragement, and begin to praise the Lord by singing His Word, we are coming against the Devil with the power of a great weapon.

Praise only has power, however, when it is coupled with the Word, the Name, and the Blood. We should examine our praise to see if we actually are launching spiritual weapons with our praise. Is our praise occupied with the declaration of the Word, the Name, or the Blood? If not, it will have no effect upon strongholds.

Singing the Word of God has great power in it. It attacks the strongholds of the Devil. We literally are resisting the Devil and can be assured that he is fleeing from us. This has great effect when it happens in a congregation. When a great body of people join together and sing the Word of God with conviction and faith, there is a corporate spiritual energy generated that attacks spiritual strongholds.

Remember what Paul said: "The weapons of our warfare are not carnal. They are mighty through God to the pulling down of strongholds." The weapon of God's Word on our lips will pull down the strongholds. It will bring miracles. It will bring sight to the blind, hearing to the deaf, deliverance to the fearful.

This is the secret of our praise and song services. We literally are launching spiritual weapons and resisting the Devil. He will flee, cancer will flee, demons will flee, the blinding thoughts of the Devil will flee. We are set free through our praise and worship. Praise is a sacrifice. It is something we must determine to do. It is an act of our will, not of our emotions. We determine to praise the Lord.

David said, "I will bless the Lord at all times, His praise shall continually be in my mouth." Every time we come into the house of God we face this golden opportunity. We can join in with the corporate praise of other believers. We can bring our hearts into unity with the Word of God that flows forth from our choruses. We can develop a divine "punch" that will smite strongholds with a mighty blow. When we resist the Devil he *does* flee from us.

This is the power that praise brings into our meetings: "By Him therefore let us offer the sacrifice of praise to God continually, that is, the fruit of our lips giving thanks to his name (Heb. 13:15)."

5

Spiritual Weapons: The Name

The paradox of Peter

Simon Peter always has been a source of curiosity to me. He was the man who made such great promises to Jesus and failed. On the night of Jesus' betrayal, Jesus told the disciples that they would become confused, scattered abroad, and would leave Him in His time of trial. But Peter boldly stated, "Though all others leave you, I will never leave you." Jesus surprisingly replied to Peter, "Peter, before the cock crows three times, you will deny me three times."

Judas betrayed Jesus to the high priests, who then sent soldiers after Jesus in Gethsemane on the Mount of Olives. Jesus was praying. He had taken Peter, James, and John with Him to the garden. He had gone a short distance from the other disciples and His heart was exceedingly grieved as He prayed and waited on His Father. When the soldiers came from the high priests, the disciples fled and Peter with them. As the soldiers took Jesus away, Peter followed afar off.

The soldiers led Jesus to Caiaphas, the high priest. Peter made his way into the palace area, and sat down among those who had actually captured Jesus. He began to warm his hands at the fire with them.

Suddenly a young girl confronted him, and said, "You were with Jesus of Galilee!" Peter denied it, and said, "I don't know what you are saying." Then another saw him, and said, "This man was with Jesus of Nazareth!" And again he denied it, this time with an oath. Then a soldier said, "Didn't I see you in the garden with Him?"

The accusations were getting close to home. Peter cursed and swore his denials. Then, Jesus turned and looked at Peter, and Peter remembered the words which Jesus had spoken. *Peter went out into the night and wept bitterly.*

As we look at this broken man crying on the night of Jesus' betrayal, we catch a view of one side of Peter's character. Here was a man who promised great things, but when it came to the crunch, he discovered that he couldn't deliver. He went out and he wept bitterly.

With that view of Peter in mind, it is very difficult to understand how fifty-two days later, on the day of Pentecost, the same man stood up and preached a sermon that confounded an entire city. Fifty-three days later he walked into the temple with John at his side and raised a man that had been lame since birth, and then preached another sermon. It is amazing. *What changed Peter? What made the difference in his life?*

He had seen Jesus crucified and also had been with the disciples when Jesus appeared after His resurrection and manifested His presence to them. I am sure this had a part in changing Peter's life. It also is true that he had waited in the upper room for ten days with the other disciples, praising God and looking for the outpouring of the Holy Spirit.

Each of these experiences, I am sure, played a part in changing Peter. But with the healing of the lame man in Acts 3, *Peter began to reveal to us what had made the difference in his life.*

The power of the Name in the early church

Peter and John had gone up to the temple at the hour of prayer, which was approximately three o'clock in the afternoon. This was the time when the priests went into the Holy Place in the temple before the Lord to offer the evening sacrifice. There was a lame man lying at the gate of the temple. He had been lame all of his life. He begged for money from Peter and John as they came in.

Peter looked at the lame man, and said to him, "Look on us." He looked at them expecting them to give him something. Then Peter said, "Silver and gold have I none; but such as I have give I thee." Peter knew that he had something to give the man. He said, "I have something, and what I have I am going to give you."

Then he said, "In the name of Jesus Christ of Nazareth rise up and walk." *Peter gave the man what he had, and what he had was the Name of Jesus.* And as soon as Peter spoke, he took the man by the right hand and lifted him up and his legs were healed.

The man leaped and walked, and praised God, running into the temple. When the people saw this, they gathered by the thousands, wondering what had happened. Then Peter stood up to preach, and the first thing he said to the people was, "Why look ye so earnestly on us, as though by our own power or holiness we had made this man to walk?"

When a man of God is used in the healing process to bring deliverance to someone, often the people look at him as though his own holiness or spirituality brought the miracle of healing. This is a normal reaction of people. They say, "My! For a man to be used of God like this! To bring healing to the sick! He certainly must be a very holy man, and he certainly must have a great amount of spiritual power!" That attitude is wrong. And Peter immediately began correcting the onlookers' thinking.

As he moved through his sermon, he revealed the key to the healing of the lame man: "And his name [that is, the Name of Jesus] through faith in his name hath made this man strong, whom ye see and know: yea, the faith which is by him hath given him this perfect soundness in the presence of you all (Acts 3:16)."

Peter makes it very clear how the lame man was healed. *He was healed with the weapon of the Name of Jesus.* Peter used the weapon of Jesus' Name when he looked at the man bound with a stronghold of lameness. Peter saw it as clear as crystal and ministered in the power and the authority of the Holy Spirit. Then he had to reemphasize this truth to the crowd and tell them that it was the Name of Jesus; faith in the Name of Jesus that had made the man strong.

In Acts 4, when Peter and John were called in by Annas and Caiaphas, the high priests, they asked them a question: "By what power, or by what name, have ye done this?" Somehow they knew that a name had brought healing to the lame man, and they wanted to know more about how and why Peter and John were using that name.

Peter said the same thing to the high priest that he had told the crowd the day before. He said, "Be it known unto you all, and to all the people of Israel, *that by the name of Jesus Christ of Nazareth,* whom ye crucified, whom God raised from the dead, even by him doth this man stand here before you whole (Acts 4:10)."

Again, Peter relates directly to the Name and tells the high priests that it was the Name that brought healing to the man. He goes on, ends up preaching them a sermon, and in Acts 4:12, he says, "Neither is there salvation in any other: for there is none other name under heaven given among men, whereby we must be saved."

When you see the awe and the respect Peter had for the Name, you begin to realize that *the Name meant something very special to the early church.* They did what they had to do for God in the authority of the Name. The Name had been delegated to them, they had received a power of attorney to use that Name, and so they went about healing the sick, they went about casting out demons, they went about raising the dead by the power of the Name.

Now, the high priests knew that they must be very cautious because of the remarkable healing of the man. They spoke to Peter and John and threatened them saying, "that they speak henceforth to no man in this Name." They wanted to stop them from the use of the Name. They realized there was an authority in the power of the Name. In Acts 4:18 it states, "And they called them, and commanded them not to speak at all nor teach in the name of Jesus."

But Peter and John said they were going to preach in that Name anyway. They went back to the other disciples, gathered the believers together, and began to praise God for the mighty miracle that God had done. They made a request in that great prayer meeting, they said, "Lord ... grant unto thy servants, that with all boldness they may speak your word, by stretching forth thine hand to heal; and that signs and wonders may be done *by the name* of thy holy child Jesus (Acts 4: 29,30)."

Notice the emphasis, "that *signs and wonders* may be done *by the name* of thy holy child Jesus." If we are going to do signs and wonders, we must use the Name. The Name of Jesus is the weapon that God has given to the Church, and the Church must use that Name with its authority and power.

In Acts 5, it is recorded how revival spread throughout Jerusalem. The high priests became so concerned at what was happening that they sent soldiers to bring in Peter and John for further questioning. The priests were very upset and they said, "Did we not straitly command you that ye should not teach in this name? and, behold, ye have filled Jerusalem with your doctrine, and intend to bring this man's blood upon us."

This is the estimate of what the early church was doing with the Name, and it came from the lips of the religious leaders of their day. The doctrine that Peter and John were preaching, the doctrine of the early church, was the doctrine of the Name. *They literally had filled the city of Jerusalem with the doctrine of the Name.*

Because there was such authority and power in the Name, the religious leaders were severely disturbed. We have lost that kind of concept of the Name of Jesus in contemporary Christianity. We do not realize that there is that kind of authority in the Name of Jesus. It has become merely a signature to our prayers rather than something that excites us and empowers us.

The high priests had the apostles beaten, and again commanded them that they should not speak in the Name of Jesus. They were trying to stop the doctrine that was filling the city. They were trying to stop the force of God that was healing the sick and bringing revival. Then the apostles "departed from the presence of the council rejoicing that they were counted worthy to suffer shame for His name" (Acts 5:41).

How important it is that we see this. They were suffering for the Name. They were suffering for the use of the Name. They were suffering for the authority of God that had been delegated to them through the power of the Name. And consequently they were being beaten because that Name had such great power on their lips. *We must see this today.*

As the revival began to spread beyond Jerusalem, Philip the evangelist, went down and preached in Samaria and Acts 8 records the story of the mighty revival that God gave him. Verse 12 states, "But when they believed Philip preaching the things concerning the kingdom of God, and the name of Jesus Christ, they were baptized both men and women."

What did Philip preach to the people in Samaria? He preached the things concerning the kingdom, and the Name of Jesus Christ. That is what Philip preached and that is why he saw such marvelous miracles as the demon oppressed freed, and the sick and lame healed. The believers left Jerusalem with one heritage, they all had the power of the Name and they knew they could use that Name. Revival followed as the Name of Jesus was used.

In Acts 9 after Saul was confronted by Jesus on the Damascus road, the Lord spoke to Ananias and told him to go to Saul, saying, "For he is a chosen vessel unto me, to *bear my name* before the Gentiles, and kings, and the children of Israel: For I will shew him how great things he must suffer *for my name's sake* (Acts 9:15, 16)."

The Lord was speaking to Ananias concerning the

future of Paul's ministry, that Paul would be preaching the power of the Name. This would be the focus of Paul's ministry. Paul would preach Jesus' Name, but first he must know that he would have to suffer many things for the Name.

Saul was converted and began preaching in the synagogue in Damascus. He preached that Jesus was the son of God. When the people heard him, they were amazed and asked, "Is not this he that destroyed them which called on this name in Jerusalem (vs. 21)?" The people knew that this was the Name that had caused the great consternation in Jerusalem, and now here is Paul in Damascus preaching and using this Name and the authority of this Name.

This raises a question about our current contemporary preaching. Why aren't we preaching the power of the Name of Jesus? Why doesn't it flow through our preaching concerning His miracles and His healing power?

There is no question as to the main theme of Peter's sermons, the main theme of Philip's sermons, the main theme of Paul's sermons. They all were wrapped around the power of the Name of Jesus. This was not a one time occurrence, it did not occur just at the beginning of their ministry.

It is impossible to get away from the conclusion, after a close examination of the book of Acts, that the early church was consumed with the power of the Name of Jesus. They took it with them everywhere they went. They used that Name, and when they used that Name, signs and wonders followed.

The names of God

It is important to understand the significance names carried in Bible times. In the culture of the Old Testament, a name often was used as a summary of character, a description of personality. It is hard to over-emphasize the importance of the name of God in the theology of the Old Testament. Names often were given prophetically to Old Testament people describing the traits they would manifest in their lives.

Isaac is a splendid example of the significance of an Old Testament name. His parents, Abraham and Sarah, had waited for many years for him to be born. When God promised his birth, Abraham fell on his face and laughed. Sarah also laughed at the promise of the son. When Isaac was born his name meant "he laughs." It suggested the joy of the aged parents as his birth brought laughter into the home. It suggests also the mocking laughter that Abraham and Sarah used years before his birth.

But we see also another dimension to the meaning. As Isaac receives this special name, God is getting the last laugh. The principle here is the fact that the name Isaac represented the character of the man to whom it was given. So also do the names of God relate very much to His character and tell us a lot about who He is.

The name *Yahweh* or *Jehovah*, speaks of God's eternal existence, but it has a dynamic quality in its meaning. It is a name of relationship, of covenant and promise. All of the Biblical theology of the Old Testament could be reduced to the meanings of the names of God. The Old Testament basically is a book about the nature and work of God. Each name God uses in His revelation to men points out certain aspects of His person and character that God wants men to understand.

The names of God offer a convenient summary of the nature of God. We praise His name whenever we praise God for His being, for His character, or for his attributes. It is important for the believer to study the names of God in the Old Testament to gain an accurate assessment of who God is.

His character revealed

In John 17:6, 26, Jesus prays His high priestly prayer, and says, *"I have manifested thy name unto the men which thou gavest me out of the world ... And I have declared unto them thy name,* and will declare it: that the love wherewith thou hast loved me may be in them, and I in them."

Jesus, in the New Testament, manifested the true dimensions of the name of God in the Old Testament unto His disciples, and actually put flesh to the theological terms that referred to God. He wanted them to see that God actually was represented in the flesh by Himself, the Christ. He manifested the name of God to His disciples by the signs and wonders He performed in their midst. Jesus came to manifest the name of God unto everyone of us. *We see in the ministry of Jesus a fulfillment of the meanings of the Old Testament names of God.*

However in dealing with any name, there are some limitations that are automatically imposed. A single name can reveal only one facet of one dimension of a person's character. If the fullness of heaven cannot contain God, how can a name fully describe Him? No name gives us complete insight into the character of God. But there are a number of names and compound names for God which reveal Him in some aspect of His character and in His dealings with mankind.

Elohim—The first word in Scripture used for God is *Elohim. Elohim* expresses the general idea of greatness and glory. It contains the idea of creative and governing power.

Yahweh—The next word for God is *Jehovah* or *Yahweh*, it speaks of His life and being. He is the Being who is absolutely self-existent, the One who in Himself possesses essential life, permanent existence. He truly is the living God.

El Shaddai—The next name is *El Shaddai*. This word is translated "almighty," and suggests the all-powerful nature of God. *Shaddai* is connected with the Hebrew word for breast, and signifies one who nourishes, supplies, and satisfies. *El Shaddai* is "one mighty to nourish, satisfy and supply." The One who sheds forth and pours out sustenance and blessing. The concept of abundance is inextricably intertwined with this great name of God.

Adonai—The next word is *Adon or Adonai*, and has a plurality of meaning. It confirms the concept of the Trinity, and is used in Psalm 110:1, "The Lord [Yahweh] said unto my Lord, [Adon]". The name speaks of ownership or mastership, and indicates that God is the owner of each member of the human family and that He demands our complete obedience to Him.

Redemptive names

Jehovah-Jireh—There are several redemptive names of God that also demand our attention. The first is *Jehovah-Jireh*. It simply means that He is the God who provides for our needs, or stated even more simply, "God will provide." That is a promise for everyone of us. When Isaac asked Abraham where the sacrifice was, Abraham said, "*Jehovah-Jireh*," God will provide. It speaks primarily of our great deliverance. This is an attribute of God's character. God brings great deliverance to His people. He is committed to provide for our needs.

Jehovah-Raphah—The next redemptive name is *Je-*

hovah-Raphah. It means Jehovah heals, "I am the God that healeth thee (Exodus 15:26)." Jehovah pledges Himself to His people to be their healer. It speaks of healing in the total sense; body, soul and spirit. The Jehovah who heals in the Old Testament is the Jesus who heals in the New. In other words, Jesus was manifesting the name of God to the disciples when He healed the sick. When He went to the cross to redeem man with the sacrifice of Himself, He was *Jehovah-Jireh;* God providing deliverance, God providing salvation.

Jehovah-Nissi—The next redemptive name is *Jehovah-Nissi,* "Jehovah my banner." The word banner can mean several things. It refers to the rod that Moses used at the Red Sea, or when he brought water out of the rock. The rod was the symbol and the pledge of God's presence and power. A banner in ancient times was not necessarily a flag, but often was a bare pole with some kind of ornament on it. It was a sign of deliverance and salvation.

This name speaks of Jehovah as lifting up a standard or a banner against the nations. When Moses' arms grew weak in the battle, the rod of God was lowered and the enemy prevailed. As long as Aaron and Hur held up his hands and the rod, then Israel prevailed.

Jehovah-Nissi means "Jehovah Himself is my banner." Jesus therefore is our banner. The banner of redemption. Like the serpent that Moses raised in the wilderness, a banner for the people, Jesus was raised up on the cross as our banner. Christ crucified is the banner for the Church. It is a sign of our victory. It is the sign of the authority that God has given to the believer. Jesus' Name represents this victory.

Jehovah-m'Kaddesh—The next redemptive name is

Jehovah-m'Kaddesh. This name is found in Leviticus 20:8, and means "Jehovah who sanctifies." To sanctify means to dedicate, to consecrate or make holy, or to set apart or separate. Holiness is the most impressive of all the attributes of God. It constitutes His fullness and His perfection. The Spirit of God is called "the Holy Spirit." It is the nature of God to make His people holy. We are commanded to sanctify ourselves as an act of freewill. Then His power makes us holy.

Jehovah-Shalom—The next redemptive name is *Jehovah-Shalom*. It means "Jehovah is Peace," and is found in Judges 6:24. Israel had been living in apostasy, and consequently had been put under bondage to the enemy. Jehovah appeared to Gideon as a deliverer and He called Himself, *Jehovah-Shalom* in confident anticipation of victory and peace. The name speaks of a harmony of relationship or reconciliation based on the completion of a transaction, the payment of a debt, the giving of satisfaction.

Jesus is called the Prince of Peace. Shalom was the most common form of greeting in Bible days and speaks also of the peace that takes place between God and man because of atonement. Being justified by faith we have peace with God. Jehovah desires peace for His people. Jesus' Name represents peace to the believer.

Jehovah-Tsidkenu—The next redemptive name is *Jehovah-Tsidkenu,* and means "Jehovah our righteousness." This name reveals two facts to us; that Jehovah is our righteousness, and our righteousness is as filthy rags. Romans 3:20 says, "there is none righteous, no not one." In order for us to be righteous, we must have the righteousness of God imputed to us. The righteousness of an innocent sufferer must be reckoned to the sinner if he is to stand before God.

This is what happened through Jesus Christ when God made Him to be sin for us, who knew no sin, that we might be made the righteousness of God in Him. His righteousness is bestowed upon us as a free gift through faith. This name reveals to us the tremendous gift that God has bestowed upon believers.

Jehovah-Rohi—The next word is *Jehovah-Rohi*, and means "Jehovah my shepherd." It is found in the first verse of Psalm 23, "The Lord is my shepherd." The primary meaning of the word shepherd is to feed or to lead to pasture, as a shepherd does his flock. Jehovah is the shepherd of His people. It carries the idea of compassionate care, God descending to lead us and to feed us as His flock. He protects the sheep from the wolves who would attack us. He provides food, pasture and water.

In John 10, Jesus is described as the Good Shepherd. When He looked upon the city of Jerusalem, his shepherd's heart was melted as He wept and cried over the city. Jesus was a complete fulfillment of this Old Testament name for God.

Jehovah-Shammah—The last redemptive name is *Jehovah-Shammah*. The meaning of the word is "Jehovah is there," and is found in Ezekiel 48:35 describing the great city of God which Ezekiel names "the Lord is there," *Jehovah-Shammah*. The idea is that God's continued presence always is amongst us. God desired to reveal this to mankind in both the tabernacle and the temple of the Old Testament. His presence always was in the midst of His people in the tabernacle.

In the same way Jesus, in the New Testament, became flesh, and brought the tabernacle among us. In the new covenant, His presence is now in believers as the living temples of God. We are the temples of the

Holy Spirit. Revelation 21:3 states, "Behold the tabernacle of God is with men, and he will dwell [or, tabernacle] with them."

A quick survey of the redemptive names of God reveals that God wants us to know Him in terms of His healing, victory, peace, sanctification, justification, preservation, guidance, and, now He always is present with us.

These names reveal the character of God. But since Jesus was a fulfillment of all the names of God from the Old Testament, *the Name of Jesus today encompasses every one of these elements.* The Name of Jesus brings healing. The Name of Jesus brings victory. The Name of Jesus brings peace. The Name of Jesus brings holiness. The Name of Jesus makes us righteous. The Name of Jesus preserves us from the Devil. The Name of Jesus is with us everywhere we go.

All of these aspects of God are encompassed in the power of the Name of Jesus. How often His Name should be on our lips.

The authority of Jesus' Name

The Bible says in Matthew 28:18, 19, "And Jesus came and spake unto them [the disciples], saying, All power [or, authority] is given unto me in heaven and in earth. Go ye therefore, and teach all nations." Mark records a parallel account in 16:15, "Go ye into all the world, and preach the gospel to every creature." Then verses 17, 18 state, "And these signs shall follow them that believe; In my name shall they cast out devils; they shall speak with new tongues ... they shall lay hands on the sick and they shall recover."

It is interesting to notice in Matthew 28, Jesus declared that all authority was given unto Him, and He then commanded or commissioned the disciples to go in that power. He said, "Go ye therefore, because I have all power, I want you to go in my name." *In that single act Jesus was granting the power of attorney to His disciples to go with His power, and to go in His Name.*

Marks' Gospel backs this up. We see here that the ability to cast out devils, to speak with new tongues, to lay hands on the sick for their recovery, is committed to the believers through the authority of the Name of Jesus. In other words, the Name has been delegated as the authority of God to the Church.

When God delegates something to us, we are made responsible for it. The name of Jesus has been given to the Church, and the Church therefore becomes responsible for the use of that name. If we do not use the Name of Jesus with faith, nothing happens. However, if we *do* use it with an awareness that this Name is representative of the power of God, then we will see the miracles of the early church.

This makes it unnecessary for us to pray to God about many of the things that we usually ask Him to do. *God literally is waiting for us to do something about the Devil.* He is waiting for us to cast out demons. Nowhere in the epistles is there any verse that encourages us to pray to God about the Devil. Jesus already has done everything that He is going to do about the Devil and his works. Jesus already has done everything He is going to do concerning sickness.

It is now up to us to use the Name. The weapons have been placed in our hands, the Church stands equipped to do the work of God. *What will we do with the Name? That is the issue.*

Using the weapon of the Name

There are many verses in the New Testament that

speak to the believers authority in resisting the Devil. 1 Peter 5:8, 9 states, "Be sober, be vigilant; because your adversary the devil, as a roaring lion, walketh about, seeking whom he may devour: Whom resist stedfast in the faith ..." *We* are told to resist the Devil. We aren't to pray to *God* to do something about the Devil. *We are to resist him.* We are to resist him in the power of the Name of Jesus.

James 4:7 states, "Submit yourselves therefore to God. Resist the devil, and he will flee from you." That word "flee" in the dictionary means "to run from as in terror." When we resist the Devil in Jesus' Name, he will run from us in terror. But notice again, *we* must resist. We do not pray to *God* to resist the Devil, *we* resist.

Ephesians 4:27 further backs up what Peter and James have said. Paul says simply, "Neither give place to the devil." Don't give the Devil any place in your life. Stand in the authority of the Name of Jesus, and demonstrate His power.

We can literally cast the Devil out by the power of the Name of Jesus. The authority of the Name of Jesus has been delegated to us as members of the body of Christ. I have seen the reality of this in a very practical way. Over the years of my ministry I have learned that Jesus' Name has great power when dealing with evil spirits.

Resisting evil spirits

I was conducting a crusade on the West Coast of the United States and we had been seeing a mighty manifestation of the miracle working power of God. In my first service in that particular crusade, a man stood up in the congregation and requested prayer for the pastor. He said, "Every time I get on my knees to pray for the pastor I feel that he is in great danger, there is going to be an attack made on his life." We prayed in response to the man's request and I put it out of my mind.

Two days later in the crusade, we had a meeting of deliverance. We came together to take authority over the evil spirits that bound the people there. When the main service was over, I continued with the deliverance service in the back room for about two hours. The Lord manifested His power in a mighty way.

As I left the deliverance service, I was walking back through the sanctuary of the church. A woman was sitting in the half-lit building, and as I walked by her, she reached out and grabbed my sleeve. She said, "You must pray with me *now!*" I was very tired. I did not feel that I could pray for her. I encouraged her to come back the next night, but she insisted. As I looked into her eyes, I was aware of the fact that she was being tormented.

I realized immediately where the source of the torment came from, and so I decided to minister to the woman. I spoke to her and informed her that I was going to cast out the evil spirit that was oppressing her. The first spirit that named itself to me, was the spirit of anger, and it came out without any problem. The next spirit that spoke to me surprised me. It did not speak in the woman's voice, but rather in a male voice. The spirit informed me that it was going to murder the pastor.

I had never encountered anything quite like this before. I informed the evil spirit that it was not going to murder the pastor, but that it was going to leave the woman. I commanded the spirit to come out in the Name of Jesus. As soon as I said the Name of Jesus, the woman began to tremble. The spirit began to shake the woman with real force. Finally, after a short time, the spirit left the woman, and she was free.

I did not discover until some time after, that she had been sitting in the sanctuary with a loaded .22 caliber pistol in her purse. She was waiting for an opportunity to shoot the pastor. She would have shot him within the next five minutes. But the Spirit of the Lord led me to her at the right time, and the deliverance of God was there for her.

I never cease to be amazed at the power and the authority in the Name of Jesus. The demons know when you know that that power is there. They will obey the authority of that Name if you know that you have the authority to use that Name. It is so important that we take time to find out the power in the Name of Jesus.

Living in senseless poverty

I am reminded of a story that I heard my father tell twenty-five years ago as I was a boy growing up in church. The story came from Charles Spurgeon, the great English preacher. Spurgeon told the story first from his pulpit in London.

A woman had been hired by a very rich man to take care of his household. She served the rich man faithfully for over twenty years. When the rich man was about to die, he called the poor woman to his bedside and thanked her for her faithfulness to him. He had no heirs, and therefore decided to be generous to the woman. He wrote something on a piece of paper and handed it to her. She was grateful for this act of rememberance on his part.

She lived in a little shack on the outskirts of the city

of London. She took the piece of paper home and pinned it up on the wall. Several years later she became sick and Spurgeon, the great preacher, was called to visit her.

After he prayed for her, he walked around the room and noticed this piece of paper on the wall. He turned to the woman and asked her about it and she told him the story. He added, "Can you read?" She said, "No. I have never been taught how to read." And then he said, "Madam, this piece of paper is a check for a great deal of money. You did not have to be living in these poor circustances. You could have been living in the finest houses in London, eating the finest food."

How true this is for many of us concerning the Name of Jesus. The Word of God tells us that by the Name we have been granted the power of attorney, for that Name has been granted to the Church. It is like a blank check that God has written and signed. And yet we have never cashed it in.

We have never taken the Name and done with it what God intended to be done with it. When we cash the check signed in the Name of Jesus, that check will be honored by God in the banks of heaven. The Devil has to answer and respond to the power of the Name of Jesus.

Over the years, I have been like the rest of God's children. I have realized that there was great power in the Name of Jesus, and yet, when I used the Name that great power did not seem to be manifested. So for years in my ministry, I did not expect to see any miraculous manifestation through the use of the Name. I was like the people Jesus spoke of in John 16:24, "Hitherto have ye asked nothing in my name: ask, and ye shall receive that your joy may be full."

All this leads us to a very practical question. *How can we come to a recognition and a realization of the power that there is in Jesus' Name?* What did Jesus mean when He gave us so many promises that related to His Name?

It says in Matthew 18:19, 20, "Again I say unto you, That if two of you shall agree on earth as touching any thing that they shall ask, it shall be done for them of my Father which is in heaven. For where two or three are gathered together in my name, there am I in the midst of them." When we are gathered together in His Name, He always is with us. When we are gathered in His Name, Jesus says to the church, "Whatsoever ye shall ask of the Father in my name, that will I do." Why then are we not seeing God's manifestation in our lives?

In Ephesians 1:17, Paul prays for the Church and he asks that the eyes of their spirits may be enlightened to the things of God. And this is where we get the understanding of the power in the Name of Jesus. It must be in our inner man. It must be down on the inside in our spirits, not just in our minds. We can read this book called the Bible and come to an intellectual understanding of the power in Jesus' Name. But that understanding must get down to our spirits.

The Name, praise, and worship

Praise and worship should play a vital part in the life of the believer in relationship to the Name of Jesus. There are many blessed choruses available to believers that relate to the power of Jesus' Name. Many of the Psalms uplift the power of the Name of Jesus: "Oh Lord, our Lord, how majestic is thy name in all the earth." What a powerful chorus to sing.

As we spend time praising the Lord, and praising the power of His Name, we are entering into spiritual warfare. Our spirit is catching the revelation of the Word of God. As we sing about the Name, our spirit catches the revelation of the Name.

As we continue to flow in this dimension we prepare ourselves for that great spiritual revelation that all of us need concerning the Name of Jesus. As we continue to sing and meditate on that Name, that revelation will come, and then when it comes, we will manifest the power of God as we have never seen it manifested before.

Praise will lead us into the mighty revelation of God concerning the Name of Jesus. Hebrews 13:15 says, "By him [Christ] therefore let us offer the sacrifice of praise to God continually, that is, the fruit of our lips giving thanks [confessing] to his name." We are to offer a sacrifice of praise to God continually.

A sacrifice involves something that is difficult to do. When things are going wrong, we are to offer a sacrifice of praise, we are to do it continually, every day of our lives. It is to be the fruit of our lips. The praise that we offer should be offered verbally, it should be offered by our lips, it should be spoken out loud.

How do we give that praise? We give thanks to His Name. That is what praise is. Praise is giving honor to the Name. Praise and worship are inextricably tied up with the power of the Name of Jesus. The sacrifice of praise will lead us into a mighty revelation of Jesus' Name.

I began this chapter with a description of Peter going out into the night weeping bitterly. What happened to the man? There is no question in my mind that he came into a personal revelation of the power of the Name of Jesus.

There are many believers who are weeping bitterly in the midnight of disease, financial bondage, divorce, demonic oppression and temptation. The Name of Jesus is the answer for us today. I pray that God will give to you a powerful revelation of Jesus' Name as your weapon. With this weapon, we will pull down strongholds.

6

Spiritual Weapons: The Blood

Several years ago, I read a story that moved me deeply. It concerned an airforce major who entered a Texas mental institution in the spring of 1959. He had been arrested for several crimes, such as robbery and forgery. He had tried to kill himself twice. His marriage had fallen apart and for years he had been drinking very heavily. Yet, just a few years before he had been one of the most promising young officers in the air- force, headed for a brilliant career.

One single momentous event turned the major's life upside down. He flew the lead plane over Hiroshima when the first atom bomb was dropped. Shortly afterward his life changed radically. In his dreams he would see throngs of Japanese men, women, and children chasing him. His life began to collapse.

The professional psychologists who treated him said that the major was subconsciously trying to pro- voke punishment from society to atone for the guilt he felt over Hiroshima. Guilt was like a cancer destroying his very soul.

Satan the accuser of the brethren

All of us are troubled by recurring guilt problems of one kind or another. For centuries, Christians have thought guilt feelings were the voice of God. In reality they result from the devil using our inner guilt feelings to frustrate and defeat us. *Satan is the accuser of the brethren.*

Most of us have been taught to think that God is speaking to us when we feel guilty and the devil is lulling us into a spirit of complacency when we feel innocent. We think that conviction is God making us miserable. Conviction simply means that God is clearly showing us our sins and admonishing us to change.

Sin consciousness has held many Christians in bondage for years. Whenever anyone preached against sin, they said, "that's me." They are constantly aware of the effects of sin in their life. They have never really come into a revelation concerning the realities of the new creation.

Man has a highly developed sin consciousness, a spiritual inferiority complex, a sense of unworthiness that dominates him. The Church has been very strong in her denunciation of sin in the believer and has consequently lacked in presenting the truth of what we are in Christ Jesus by faith. We hear condemnation preached from the pulpit, rather than the declaration of our righteousness in Christ Jesus.

Guilt is one of the most powerful psychological forces in a human being. Satan, master strategist that he is, knows how to manipulate us because of our guilt feelings. My major problems as a young man growing up were problems of overwhelming guilt. Satan knew me better than I knew myself. He knew how to trigger a sense of sin consciousness in me that constantly robbed me of spiritual victory.

My father used to tell a story many years ago that carries a tremendous message. A minister had a friend who was the caretaker of a zoo. One day, they imported a new snake from the continent of Africa. The zoo keeper invited the minister to come and watch a strange phenomenon. He took a little sparrow, opened the door of the snake cage, and threw the sparrow in. When the little bird saw the snake, it was terrified and it fluttered around in the farthest corner away fom the snake.

The snake did not chase the bird. He simply coiled in the corner and fastened his eyes upon the bird. The minister was intrigued to watch. The little bird suddenly stopped its fluttering. It was slowly being hypnotized by the snake. Soon the little bird hopped down off the perch, the snake opened its mouth, and the little bird jumped in.

Paul talked about the mystery of iniquity. Sin and guilt have a hypnotic quality about them. As long as our eyes are fastened upon them, we are unable to break away from them. Most of us are hypnotized by the things we are trying to stop because we are looking inside of ourselves for willpower to say no.

The sin treadmill

Many Christians find themselves involved in what I call the sin treadmill. We come under the preaching of the gospel. We are convicted for our sin and guilt. We confess before the Lord, sometimes with strong crying, and say, "Lord forgive me this one time and I promise you I will never do it again."

We go along for a certain amount of time, perhaps two weeks, a month, and everything seems fine. Then we are caught on the blind side and we trip up and fall. We are back committing this sin again and we feel so worthless. We come back to God and say, "Lord, forgive me just one more time." But even as we pray the prayer, there is a certain sense of hopelessness and helplessness inside. We have tried so many times and yet we continue to fail.

I recently read a survey conducted in which 500 people were asked to answer the question, "What do you experience when you are feeling guilty?" Their answers fell immediately into three categories. First, a fear of punishment. Second, a feeling of depression, worthlessness, and lowered self-esteem. Third, a feeling of isolation and rejection.

Where did these feelings come from? Consider for a moment what happens when a child misbehaves. What did your parents do when you failed to live up to their ideals? Usually they would react in one of the following manners. They would punish you in anger or frustration, or they would shame you for your misbehavior, or they would subtly reject you for the failure sending you to your room.

When we grow up, we transfer these parental reactions to God. We feel that God is saying to us, "shame on you, you know better than that. After all I have done for you, how could you hurt Me this way." Or we immediately expect Him to withdraw His presence from us, much like we felt when we were sent to our room.

The Devil begins to monopolize our feelings of guilt and that makes the problem worse. When we find ourselves in this kind of spiritual state, it is almost impossible to have a strong faith in God. 1 John 3:21 says, "If our heart condemn us not, then have we confidence toward God." Guilt of this great intensity makes us miserable. We don't want to pray. We can't believe that God will heal us. We have no faith for answers for financial problems. And most important of all, *we find that we cannot praise the Lord.*

We say to ourselves, "how can someone as bad as I

am lift up his voice in praise to the Father? I cannot do it. I am a hypocrite. God won't hear me." And so we go around and around—sinning, feeling guilty, repenting, then doing it all over again.

Guilt reactions

Our reactions to this kind of guilt are fairly uniform. Some people simply give up. They have accepted the Devil's accusations. They feel themselves spiritually and emotionally drained. They have accepted the fact that they are "no good". And with this lowered sense of spiritual self-esteem, they plod on through life.

Other people get angry. They decide they are going to fight back against whoever makes the rules. This is how I reacted to God as a teenager. I felt my spiritual inferiority so deeply that I began to fight back. I wanted to say to my parents and the leadership of the Church, "I'll show you that you can't shove that down my throat." And then I would do something radical to underline my anger.

Others react differently again. They begin to rationalize their guilt. They say, "I am not really so bad as all of that. I know someone else in this church who does a lot worse things than I do." This reaction takes us back to the garden of Eden. When Adam and Eve sinned, God came to fellowship with them in the cool of the evening. They were afraid and hid themselves. They sewed an apron of leaves to cover their nakedness. This was man's first religious act before God.

Man's religion has been covering his nakedness ever since. However, God would not accept the leaves as a covering and He Himself covered their nakedness with the skins of animals. Innocent blood had to be shed to cover man's sin.

When God questioned Adam concerning the sin,

Adam pointed his finger at Eve and said, "the woman that you gave me, she's the problem." When God looked at Eve, she pointed at the serpent and blamed him. Man began to "pass the buck" for sin in the garden and he's been doing the same thing ever since.

Other people react differently again. They have learned that the psychological pressure of guilt can be relieved by asking God for forgiveness. This is a subtle reaction and very dangerous.

They are like a child who is caught with his hand in the cookie jar. He's not really sorry for his action. He's only sorry that he got caught. They ask God to forgive them, but they don't really intend to change their behavior. They will be back tomorrow doing the same thing. I call this spiritual cosmetic surgery, but it ultimately ends up trying to manipulate the grace of God.

The fifth kind of reaction, and the right reaction, is constructive sorrow as discussed in 2 Corinthians 7:9,10. It is the only reaction to wrong doing that produces lasting change for the right reasons. The Greek word for repentance actually means to change your mind; to do an about face. Constructive sorrow produces a positive change in behavior. The Holy Spirit must bring about this kind of Godly sorrow.

Is there an answer to guilt? Can we ever know a position of spiritual victory in our Christian life? How can we ever be acceptable in God's eyes?

Righteousness in the gospel

The answer to men's guilt is found in the essence of the gospel message. Paul says in Romans 1:16, "For I am not ashamed of the gospel of Christ: for it is the power of God unto salvation to every one that believeth; to the Jew first, and also to the Greek." The next verse is a significant one. "For therein [in the gospel] is the righteousness of God revealed from faith to faith: as it is written, The just shall live by faith."

These two verses make one fundamental truth very clear. *The gospel is given to us as a revelation of righteousness.* The righteousness of God is revealed to the Church in the gospel. Understand that truth and you will realize the power of God.

If you have not understood your righteousness in the gospel, then you have not understood the gospel. Many of us have been believing a half-gospel for years. We have never been willing to take our stand in righteousness as the Word of God reveals it to us. The Bible says the righteous, or the just, shall live by his faith. Our living must be predicated on our righteousness. Only then can we live correctly.

2 Corinthians 5:21 makes it very clear, "For he [God] has made him [Christ] to be sin for us, who knew no sin; that we might be made the righteousness of God in him." This verse is really a divine exchange. God by His nature is righteous and holy. But we by nature are sinful and this creates a problem. How can a holy God fellowship with a sinful man? Because His fundamental nature is to love us, God desires to have fellowship with us.

This is the innate challenge of redemption. Legally God has to make us as righteous as He is Himself in order to have fellowship. This verse explains it so clearly. God made Jesus to be sin with our sin, so that we might be made righteous with His righteousness. God has given us this gift of righteousness no matter how we feel—guilty, depressed, isolated, worthless. God has made us righteous in spite of how we perform. *You are as righteous as Jesus Christ is righteous.*

There comes a time when you must declare it and say, "I am righteous." God does not grade us on the curve. There is no such thing as being 67% righteous. We are either 100% righteous or we are not righteous at all. This imputed righteousness means that every time God looks at me, now that I am His child, He doesn't see my own righteousness which falls far short of His perfection. He sees me through the "grid" of Jesus' righteousness. Therefore, I am as acceptable to Him as His Son Jesus is, regardless of my daily performance.

This righteousness is given to me freely and completely the moment I place faith in Christ as Savior. It can't be added to, or improved upon, by God or man. I receive this righteousness strictly on the basis of faith alone.

So few believers really understand the depth of righteousness and they mistake the condemnation of Satan, fellow believers, and their own conscience as being from God. They think it is God that is accusing them of their sin.

If you condemn yourself for a weak Christian life, you are bound also to have a critical view of others. We hate most in others what we hate about ourselves. Yet if Christ doesn't condemn your brother, but accepts him on the basis of having declared him righteous, then what right do I have to condemn him. *If we aren't straight in our thinking on the subject of righteousness, nothing else will work right in our Christian lives.*

Romans 10:10 says, "For with the heart man believeth unto righteousness." You must believe with your heart. The Devil will tell you that you are a liar. He will use all of the psychological guilt mechanisms from your past. He will say that you are rotten to the core; that God is going to judge you for your sins; that you are not nearly good enough to serve the Lord.

But our declaration has to be, "I am righteous." And if we stay with it, if we continue to confess it with our lips, God will open our spiritual eyes to the revelation of the truth. We will begin to see ourselves being the righteousness of God in Christ. Then Satan will have lost his ground of accusation. The Devil is defeated when the believer understands what his righteousness means.

Most people ask several questions at this point. "How can I practically move into the truth of my righteousness? How can I reinforce it in my life on a daily basis? How can I break out of this cycle of sin? How can I get away from my psychological guilt? Is it possible to live with a continual awareness of the righteousness of Christ in my life?"

The Blood and our righteousness

There is an answer to these questions. *The answer is found in the Blood of Jesus Christ.* This is where the power of the believer's weapon comes into play. Romans 5:9 says, "Much more then, being now justified [made righteous] by his blood, we shall be saved from wrath through him." *This verse declares that we are made righteous by the Blood of Jesus.*

This is a fundamental truth. In order to understand the reality of our righteousness, we must understand the meaning of the Blood. This is where the believer moves into spiritual warfare. This is where he learns to attack the accuser of the brethren. It is a daily battle, but it is one that God wants him to win.

In Revelation 12:10, 11, we read, "And I heard a loud voice saying in heaven, Now is come salvation, and strength, and the kingdom of our God, and the power of his Christ: for the accuser of our brethren is cast down, which accused them before our God day and night. And they overcame him by the blood of the Lamb, and by the word of their testimony; and they loved not their lives unto the death."

This scripture is speaking about a future event; a time when the believers will cast the Devil down by the power of the Blood and the word of their testimony. However, it does illustrate spiritual principles that are operative in your life and mine today.

Notice the believers overcame the Devil by the use of spiritual weapons. The weapon used in this case was the Blood of the Lamb. The spiritual launching vehicle was the word of their testimony. How does this relate to us today? Believers are to overcome Satan's guilt accusations by the Blood and the word of their testimony. *What this verse means is that we must testify to what the Word says that the Blood of Jesus does for us.* This testimony must be given on a regular basis.

The key to your realization of righteousness lies in your declaration concerning the Blood. You must testify with your mouth to the power of that Blood, and you must do it regularly.

The Blood

We have become overfamiliar with the term the Blood of Jesus. Let me explain what that phrase means. In a natural birth, blood cells in the child come from both parents. Neither male spermatozoan, nor the female ovum, has any blood in itself. The new life begins to develop when these two come together in the fallopian tube at the time of conception. The blood type of the new child is determined at the moment of conception and is protected by the placenta from any flow of the mother's blood into the fetus.

When Jesus was conceived in the womb of Mary, the Holy Spirit planted the life of God's Son in Mary's womb. Since conception did not occur naturally in the fallopian tube, Mary did not supply any of her Adamic blood into the spotless Lamb of God. The blood type of Jesus Christ, God's Son, was pure and precious. Jesus' Blood was free from the Adamic stain of sin and was not contaminated. The Blood that flowed in His veins was perfect. *Jesus had the Blood of God.*

It is important to ask at this point, what happened to the Blood of Jesus? Why is it so powerful today? Hebrews 9:12 gives us an answer. "Neither by the blood of goats and calves, but by his own blood he entered in once into the holy place, having obtained eternal redemption for us."

After Jesus died, this verse indicates that there was a time when He ascended to God the Father and brought His Blood into the Holy of Holies before God in Heaven. He placed His Blood on the altar before God. That Blood is there today, as freshly slain as it was 2,000 years ago when Jesus Christ died on the cross. That is an objective theological fact. The Blood of Jesus Christ is on the altar before God. It is that Blood that cleanses me from sin.

Now, it is one thing for me to understand that fact, but I still have a subjective problem. I need the Blood applied to my address every day that I live. Today I need to know the cleansing action of the Blood by faith. I need to establish my righteousness on the authority of the Blood right now. How do I make this happen?

In Exodus 12, we have a beautiful analogy of how to make the Blood work in our lives. Israel had been in bondage to Pharoah for 400 years. Moses had gone to Pharoah commanding him to let God's people go. Pharoah refused. Moses commanded ten various plagues that came upon the land of Egypt. The tenth plague was now to be fulfilled. The death angel would move through the land of Egypt and every house that was not covered by the blood of an innocent lamb would be smitten. That meant that the oldest boy child in the home would be slain by the death angel.

God gave Moses a plan to protect the children of Israel. He told them that they were to slay a lamb for every family. Then after the lamb was slain they were to collect the blood of the lamb in a basin. They were then to take the blood and sprinkle it on the two sideposts of the door and the lintel over top of the door.

The believers' testimony

There was one problem, however. How did they get the blood from the basin to the doorpost? This is exactly the question that we ask concerning the Blood of Jesus on the altar before God in Heaven. How can I get it applied to the doorposts of my life? God's plan was simple. He instructed them to take a weedlike herb called hyssop. The hyssop was dipped into the blood and then the blood was sprinkled onto the doorposts.

In Revelation 12:11, the Bible says that the believers overcame the Devil by the Blood of the Lamb and by the word of their testimony. *Our testimony is like the hyssop that daily applies the Blood to our lives.* Our testimony must take what the Word says about the Blood on a daily basis and apply it to the doorpost of our lives spiritually. We must declare before the Devil, before God, and before ourselves what the Blood does for us. In this way, the ongoing work of the Blood becomes a faith reality to us and we can live in the power of that Blood.

We must, with our testimony or witness, declare

the effective work of the Blood on our behalf. When you do this, you discover that the Devil is afraid of a Christian who sees the Blood in this manner. Because he knows he is dealing with a believer who has understood his righteousness and who is standing firm in his faith.

At this point, *the Blood becomes a spiritual weapon.* It becomes a great power against the invasion of the Devil. It stops his most powerful tool of oppression. Praise the Lord! The accuser of the brethren must shut up. He has no ground of accusation in us because we are cleansed by the Blood.

The believer, however, must focus on the power of the Blood. When we get our eyes off of the sin that doth so easily beset us and get our eyes focused on the power of the Blood and the fact that we are made righteous through that Blood, we will find ourselves standing in a position of spiritual victory.

It is important, therefore, at this point to meditate on what the Word says that the Blood does for us. What does scripture tell us about the Blood of Jesus Christ? There are so many verses that we could apply at this point. Here are a few that will help you. I use these verses devotionally almost every day of my life. I have learned the power of giving testimony to what the Word says about the Blood. I would encourage you to make a devotional habit of using these verses in your own life.

The first verse is Ephesians 1:7, "In whom we have redemption through his blood, the forgiveness of sins, according to the riches of His grace." A close examination of this verse reveals that there are two things that come through the Blood of Jesus. The first is redemption. The second is the forgiveness of sins.

Redemption is the work of Jesus Christ on our behalf to cancel out the debt of sin and to release us from slavery to Satan and the sin nature. Forgiveness is a truth of scripture that reveals that God has forgiven us all our sins—past and present. And He has blotted them out of His own memory forever. They will never be brought up against us again.

Our declarations

On the basis of Ephesians 1:7, I make the following two declarations:

1. **"According to Ephesians 1:7, by the Blood of Jesus, I am redeemed, bought back out of the hand of the Devil."**

2. **"According to Ephesians 1:7, by the Blood of Jesus, all my sins are completely forgiven."**

The next verse is 1 John 1:7, "But if we walk in the light, as He is in the light, we have fellowship one with another, and the blood of Jesus Christ his Son cleanseth us from all sin." The word cleanses in this verse is in the continuing present tense in the Greek. It means that the Blood of Jesus is cleansing us now. On the basis of this verse, I make the following declaration:

3. **"According to 1 John 1:7, the Blood of Jesus Christ, God's Son, continually cleanses me from all sin."**

The next verse is Romans 5:9, "Much more then, being now justified (made righteous) by his blood, we shall be saved from wrath through him." This verse declares that the Blood of Jesus makes us righteous. I have already dealt with righteousness in this chapter. On the basis of this verse, I make the following declaration:

4. **"According to Romans 5:9, by the Blood of Jesus, I am justified, made righteous just as if I**

had never sinned."

The next verse is Hebrews 13:12, "Wherefore Jesus also, that he might sanctify the people with his own blood, suffered without the gate." The Bible declares here that we are sanctified or set apart by the Blood of Jesus. I make the following declaration on the basis of this verse:

> 5. **"According to Hebrews 13:12, by the Blood of Jesus, I am sanctified, made holy, set apart unto God."**

The next verse is 1 Corinthians 6:19, 20, "What? know ye not that your body is the temple of the Holy Ghost which is in you, which ye have of God, and ye are not your own? For ye are bought with a price ..." Notice the phrase, "ye are bought with a price." The price or ransom paid for us was the precious Blood of Jesus Christ. Our body is the temple of the Holy Spirit because of the Blood. On the basis of this verse, I make the following declaration:

> 6. **"According to 1 Corinthians 6:19, 20, my body is the temple of the Holy Spirit, redeemed, forgiven, cleansed, made righteous, and sanctified. Therefore, Satan has no place in me and no power over me. I renounce him and loose myself from him by the Blood of Jesus."**

It is at this point in spiritual warfare that praise and worship becomes necessary. It is impossible to declare the power of the Blood of Jesus in your life without sensing a spirit of praise rise up on the inside of you. Praise to God is released by a sense of righteousness that comes through the cleansing of the Blood.

A consistent daily declaration and testimony concerning the Blood will invariably move you into the areas of praise. I have found it so helpful to find choruses that declare my righteousness through the Blood of Jesus. As I sing these choruses daily, I reinforce and testify to myself and particularly to the accuser that I truly am righteous.

Powerful praise must find its foundation in the cleansing of the Blood. The two go together so naturally. The Blood is the weapon, praise is the launching rocket.

We need more songs concerning the Blood. We need more songs concerning our righteousness. Our daily testimony concerning the Blood can be done so easily in the form of a praise chorus. May God reveal to you the power of the Blood. Then may your praise, through the Blood, pull down the Devil's strongholds in your life.

7

Spiritual Launching Rockets

We have closely examined the meaning of the word "stronghold" and have discovered that strongholds are very active in the lives of God's children. They attempt to pull us down, to make us sick, to bind us with satanic oppression. They endeavor to destroy our marriages and our homes and to put us into financial and other kinds of bondage.

However, we've also learned that the weapons of our warfare are mighty through God to pull down these strongholds (2 Cor. 10:4).

When the Word of God confronts a stronghold, it will tear that stronghold down. When the Name of Jesus is brought to bear against the stronghold, the Name of Jesus will prevail. When the Blood of Jesus is brought to bear against a stronghold by the word of our testimony, that stronghold will be overcome. It is easily understood that our weapons are mighty through God to the pulling down of strongholds.

Putting warheads on our rockets

Therefore, if strongholds have been established in the second heaven, and if they manifest themselves in physical ways in our bodies and lives, *how can we get our weapons into action against strongholds in the heavenlies?*

The Word of God is a weapon, as is the Name and the Blood, but we must put them into action against strongholds. *How do we get them to the point of attack?* An example from contemporary warfare can help us understand the importance of spiritual launching rockets.

If our country were to enter into a nuclear conflict with another country, one of the first priorities for both nations would be the launching of intercontinental ballistic missles (ICBMs). These huge rockets can travel multiplied thousands of miles and destroy a target with pinpoint accuracy.

It is important, however, that we make a distinction in the rocket itself, and the warhead, which it carries. The power for explosion, the power for destruction, is in the warhead. The rocket simply is a vehicle which carries the warhead to the target. If we were to launch a rocket that did not carry a warhead, it would create a minor explosion when it hit the ground. However, if that rocket carried a warhead, it would obliberate an entire city and much of the surrounding countryside. The power for destruction is in the warhead and not in the rocket.

This is true also in the area of spiritual warfare. God's power for spiritual warfare lies in the Word, the Name, and the Blood. However, these "warheads" must be "launched" into the conflict. And God has given to the Church several launching rockets, spiritual ICBMs, that carry these weapons. They do not have power in themselves, but they carry the power of the warheads. *The four primary spiritual launching rockets are: prayer, preaching, testimony, and, praise and worship.*

The ICBM of prayer

There is no question that prayer has great power when it is carrying a spiritual weapon. Prayer receives it's power from the weapon that is used. When we pray the Word, when we pray the Name, when we pray the Blood, there is great power in the prayer. However, prayer that prays vain repetitions has no power whatsoever.

Prayer is a spiritual launching rocket. It is a transportation vehicle that carries our weapons to the point of attack.

It often has been said that prayer is the greatest force in the universe. This is no exaggeration. Prayer carries the very force and power of God. Jeremiah 33:3 says, "Call unto me, and I will answer thee, and shew thee great and mighty things, which thou knowest not."

God says in effect, that if we will pray, He will work. If we will seek His face in prayer, He will bring to pass great and mighty things. It is an amazing thing to realize that God has limited Himself. If we will not pray, to put it bluntly, He will not work. This is one of the deep mysteries of God, but it is, nonetheless, a fact.

The Bible, which is the textbook on prayer, bears eloquent witness to this fact. If God is to work great and mighty things in the affairs of men and nations, then men must pray. Prayer has such incredible potential that it lays beyond the imagination of men.

When a Christian prays, his ability to achieve is multiplied a thousand-fold. On our knees in prayer we can help missionaries in the most remote corners of the world. We can send divine help to prisoners in

America. We can minister to the ghettos of our great cities. There is no barrier of time or space with God. As Moses stretched his rod on God's behalf over Egypt, the church stretches forth Christ's authority over the nations and their rulers by prayer.

The first thing God's people are to pray for is their government. Most Christians never pray for the government. Yet in 1 Timothy 2:1-4, Paul writes:

1 I exhort therefore, that, first of all, supplications, prayers, intercessions, and giving of thanks, be made for all men;
2 For kings, and for all that are in authority; that we may lead a quiet and peaceable life in all godliness and honesty.
3 For this is good and acceptable in the sight of God our Saviour;
4 Who will have all men to be saved, and to come unto the knowledge of the truth."

When we pray for government, we are to pray that we may lead a quiet and peaceable life. Why? Because God wants *all men to be saved.* The connection between good government and the ability to preach the Gospel is obvious. Good government makes it possible for men to preach freely the message of Salvation to other men. It guarantees civil liberty and protects the freedom of speech.

The laws of prayer

There are several Scriptural laws which govern praying. First is the law of boldness stated in Hebrews 10:19, "Having therefore, brethren, boldness to enter into the holiest by the blood of Jesus." We have the right to be bold because the Blood of Jesus is on the altar before God.

Another law of prayer also is illustrated in this verse, and that is the law of the Blood. Prayer that is offered on the foundation of faith in the Blood has power. The cleansing of the Blood is basic to our approach to God.

A third law of prayer is the law of faith: "But without faith it is impossible to please him: for he that cometh to God must believe that he is, and that he is a rewarder of them who diligently seek Him (Hebrews 11:6)."

Another law of prayer is the law of right relations, as stated in Mark 11:24, 25, "Therefore I say unto you, What things soever ye desire, when ye pray, believe that ye receive them and ye shall have them. And when ye stand praying, forgive, if ye have ought against any: that your Father also which is in heaven may forgive your trespasses."

The fifth law of prayer is the law of God's will: 1 John 5:14, 15, "And this is the confidence that we have in him, that, if we ask any thing according to his will, he heareth us: And if we know that he hear us, whatsoever we ask, we know that we have the petitions that we desired of him." God answers any prayer that it is prayed in His will.

There also is the law of the Holy Spirit in prayer as stated in Romans 8:26, "Likewise the Spirit also helpeth our infirmities: for we know not what we should pray for as we ought: but the Spirit itself maketh intercession for us with groanings which cannot be uttered."

The seventh law of prayer is the law of praise. "I will bless the Lord at all times," David said, "His praise shall continually be in my mouth (Psalm 34:1)."

There also is the law of right motives in praying. James says, "Ye ask, and receive not, because ye ask amiss, that ye may consume it upon your lusts (Ja. 4:3)."

There is one element of prayer that is vital in spiritual warfare, and that is the prayer of binding and loosing. In Matthew 16, Jesus responded to Simon Peter for his announcement that He was the Christ, the Son of the living God. Jesus said:

> 17 Blessed art thou, Simon Bar-jona: for flesh and blood hath not revealed it unto thee, but my father which is in heaven.
> 18 And I say also unto thee that thou art Peter, and upon this rock I will build my church; and the gates of hell shall not prevail against it.
> 19 And I will give unto thee the keys of the kingdom of heaven: and whatsoever thou shalt bind on earth shall be bound in heaven: and whatsoever thou shalt loose on earth shall be loosed in heaven.

This does not mean that the gates of hell will come crashing against the Church, but rather, that the Church will come against the gates of hell, and the gates will collapse.

Again, in Matthew 18:18-20, Jesus said:

> 18 Verily I say unto you, Whatsoever ye shall bind on earth shall be bound in heaven: and whatsoever ye shall loose on earth shall be loosed in heaven.
> 19 Again I say unto you, that if two of you shall agree on earth as touching any thing that they shall ask, it shall be done for them of my Father which is in heaven.
> 20 For where two or three are gathered together *in my name*, there am I in the midst of them.

The authority of the believer in prayer is something that most of us never grasp. God literally is saying to us, "What you bind on earth already has been bound in heaven." The responsibility for binding is ours. We must stand in the victory that already has been accomplished for us in Christ Jesus.

The prayer of binding and loosing is a prayer related directly to the Word of God. The authority to pray that prayer comes from scripture itself. Again, the Word of God is a weapon that prayer launches into action against the power of the enemy. The prayer of binding and loosing must be prayed in the Name of Jesus. That is the one weapon that Satan yields to. He is terrified of believers who stand in the power of the Name of Jesus.

The prayer of binding and loosing must be launched on the authority of the shed Blood of Jesus. That blood gives great authority to that kind of praying. The Devil knows if we understand the power of the Word, the Name, and the Blood. When we take authority in prayer on the basis of our three weapons, the results will be immediately apparent.

The ICBM of preaching

The next spiritual launching rocket is preaching. Preaching is a great tool that God has given to the church for the launching of spiritual weapons. Paul counseled Timothy in (2 Tim. 4:2), "Preach the word."

That says it as simply as it can be said. When a preacher stands up and preaches the Word of God, he is launching the Word of God as a weapon. His preaching is a rocket that carries the power of the Word to the target. When we preach the Gospel, we should expect to pull down strongholds. We should expect our preaching to produce miraculous results. We should launch our preaching with faith.

We can better understand the importance and power of preaching in Scripture by examining the life of the great preacher, Paul the Apostle. Paul was a preacher from the moment of his conversion until the day he died.

Paul was commissioned from the beginning of his ministry to take the Name of Jesus before the Gentiles, and before kings. Acts 9:20, 21 states, "And straightway he preached Christ in the synagogues, that he is the Son of God. But all that heard him were amazed, and said; Is not this he that destroyed them which called on this name in Jerusalem?" Notice again the Name of Jesus. Paul's preaching from the beginning was focused around the Name of Jesus.

He continually preached that righteousness came to the believer who was willing to confess the power of the Name of Jesus. Paul knew that righteousness came through the Blood of Jesus (Romans 5:9). Paul realized that righteousness itself is predicated on the cleansing of the Blood of Jesus. In other words he had to preach the cleansing of the Blood in order for righteousness to be a focus of his ministry.

It is obvious that the Name of Jesus had a great power in Paul's preaching. In the declaration of salvation, Paul said, "for whosoever shall call upon the name of the Lord, shall be saved." What a powerful launching rocket preaching becomes when focused on the power of the Word, the Name, and the Blood.

The ICBM of testimony

The next spiritual launching rocket is testimony. Revelation 12:11 declares, "And they [the believers] overcame him [the Devil], by the blood of the Lamb, and by the word of their testimony." That word "testimony" in the Greek is used interchangably with the word "witness" in the King James Bible. To testify literally means to give witness. They have exactly the same meaning and are the same word in the Greek.

When you testify as a witness in a court of law, you are asked to tell only what you saw and what you heard. You are to speak from direct personal experience, not from opinion or presumption. The testimony or witness is a basic element of our justice system, and it is something that God uses as a launching rocket in His kingdom.

There is a unique place in the kingdom of God for personal testimony. Personal testimony is literally a spiritual launching rocket that sends forth the power of our weapons; the Word, the Name, and the Blood.

For years I have believed that every Christian is called upon to give testimony to what God has done in his life. We are not called to be preachers, but simply are called to give witness. In Acts 1:8, Jesus said "ye shall receive power, after that the Holy Ghost is come upon you: and ye shall be witnesses."

The baptism of the Holy Spirit is given to make us a witness. It is the desire of the Holy Spirit within you and me to launch the spiritual rocket of our testimony. If our testimony is centered around the Word, the Name and the Blood, then great power will be unleashed.

Notice the latter part of Acts 1:8, "and ye shall be witnesses unto me in Jerusalem, in all Judaea, in Samaria, and unto the uttermost part of the earth." Our testimony, our witness, is to reach around the world.

It is testimonies of believers that will bring worldwide revival. This is the reason for being baptized in the Holy Spirit. We were not given the Holy Spirit so that we could talk in tongues, or have an exuberant emotional experience, or separate ourselves from others in the body of Christ because of a distinctive doctrine. The power of the Spirit is given to make us a witness, to launch our rockets.

If someone says God doesn't heal today, and you testify to the fact that He healed you of this disease or that disease, that settles the argument. Everyone will listen to a personal testimony. Many of us are cheated out of our testimony because we don't think it is as sensational as someone else's. That is the Devil's lie. Every person's testimony is a witness to God's power.

If you examine the New Testament you will find that Paul gives his own personal testimony on several different occasions. Paul knew the importance of the launching power of repeated personal testimony.

When I traveled with Oral Roberts, almost every time I heard him preach the Gospel, he shared his personal testimony. He told the story of collapsing on a gymnasium floor playing basketball at seventeen years of age. He told of how his sister spoke to him and said, "Oral, God is going to heal you." He told the story of how he was healed and came into a manifestation of the power of God.

I used to ask myself, "Why does he continually tell the story? Doesn't he know that everyone has heard it many, many times?" Only as I began to study the power of personal testimony, did I become aware of what Oral Roberts was doing.

Kenneth Hagin does the same thing. I have heard him speak on many different occasions. Almost every time he speaks, I hear him recount the story of being bedfast at sixteen years of age, in the east bedroom of his home in McKinney, Texas. I can almost tell the story as well as he can. And again the question was always in my mind, "Why does he continue to tell the story almost every time he preaches to the people?" Only when I realized the power of personal testimony, did I realize why.

There is nothing more real in all the world than to recount what God has done specifically for you. To testify to the power of God in your life. Everyone who has been forgiven from sin has a powerful testimony. You have a testimony. I have a testimony. When we launch our testimony, we unleash a spiritual law and that law is just as true and unbreakable as the laws of physics.

When we testify to Christ, when we uplift Jesus according to John 12:31-32, our testimony will draw men to Christ. They may not be saved, but they will be drawn by the Holy Spirit. There is a drawing power in testimony.

What a powerful launching rocket testimony is in a church. I believe that when the church commits itself to giving testimony to the power of the Word, the Name, and the Blood, we will reach the entire world with the Gospel within a few years. But that commitment to testimony must come on the part of all believers.

The ICBM of praise & worship

The fourth spiritual launching rocket is praise and worship. Each one of the spiritual launching rockets is a singular act of the individual. Prayer is an individual thing. Preaching is done by just a single person. Each of us must have a testimony. Praise and worship also is a personal thing, but it can become corporate as part of the body of Christ within the congregation.

When praise and worship is loosed by a group, there is a tremendous amount of power generated. Psalms 22:3 says that God inhabits the praises of His people. When we praise God together, God inhabits our praise. Because corporate praise involves the power of agreement, the power of coming into harmony, there is a tremendous spiritual energy generated.

The power of the mouth

All four spiritual launching rockets have something to do with the mouth. We pray with our mouth, we preach with our mouth, we testify with our mouth and we praise and worship with our mouth. *The mouth is the center of spiritual warfare for the universe.* With our mouths, we launch the weapons of God — the Word, the Name, and the Blood.

But we can also launch the weapons of the enemy as well. When we gossip, backbite, criticize, and judge the lives of others, we launch the Devil's weapons. But if we choose rather, to launch the Word, the Name, and the Blood through our prayer, our preaching, our testimony, and our praise and worship, then literally we become responsible for launching the weapons of God.

God has tied the spiritual power of the universe to the human mouth. That is why it is so important that we recognize the place of the tongue. It's significant to me that when believers receive the baptism of the Holy Spirit, they begin to speak with other tongues. If our mouth is the center of spiritual warfare, then what the Holy Spirit wants to capture in our lives is the power of our mouth. That is why speaking in tongues relates directly to spiritual warfare.

In Acts 2, when the believers in the Upper Room were baptized with the Holy Spirit, they began to speak and magnify the wonderful works of God. What were they doing? They were praising the Lord. Their prayer language was leading them into praise.

When Cornelius and his household were filled with the Holy Spirit in Acts 10, they also began to magnify the Lord by speaking in other tongues. When we speak in tongues, we magnify God. We bring praise unto the Lord. We enter into the elements of spiritual warfare. We begin to launch spiritual weapons that we cannot see. Even though our mind may not be cognizant of the power of our prayer, we are nonetheless launching spiritual weapons.

From darkness to light with praise

It is very important to notice how praise ranks as a spiritual launching rocket along with prayer, preaching, and testimony. It was the means by which Paul and Silas launched their spiritual weapons against the strongholds that would have kept them incarcerated in prison.

Paul said in 2 Corinthians 10:4, "Our weapons are mighty through God to the pulling down of strongholds." And in the jail in Philippi, the man practiced what he preached. He literally pulled down the strongholds by the power of praise. He launched his weapons and the foundations of the prison were shaken (Acts 16:19-40).

There is a great message here for all of us. In fact, the story is also a parable. In the life of many people, things are dark. It is midnight. Midnight because of sickness and disease, midnight because of the oppression of the Devil, midnight because of a problem in a marriage, midnight because of overwhelming temptations, midnight because of financial bondage.

But Acts 16:25 declares, "At midnight Paul and Silas prayed, and sang praises." In the midst of the darkness, in the midst of the hurt, in the midst of the pain, they praised God. They launched their spiritual rockets armed with the warheads of the Word, the Name, and the Blood. They offered a sacrifice of praise, and their prison, the stronghold, was shaken, and they were freed. This is what praise and worship can do for us today.

8

Thanksgiving, Praise, And Worship

Many Christians find themselves using the words thanksgiving, praise, and worship interchangeably. However, we must be aware of the fact that there are different meanings for the words. Thanksgiving is distinct from praise which is distinct from worship. Thanksgiving relates to God's deeds, what He has done. Praise relates to God's character, who He is. Worship relates directly to God's holiness.

1. The meaning and purpose of thanksgiving

Thanksgiving is a New Testament term. Praise is an Old Testament word. The New Testament Scriptures regularly speak of thanksgiving that can be done in one's heart and in private, and these references of course, are made in the Greek language.

All of the Hebrew terms from the Old Testament for praise have a connotation of being public and open. Thanksgiving may be silent and private, but praise is vocal and public. Thanksgiving occurs when we breathe a prayer of thanks to God. Praise occurs when we thank God publicly, telling others of what He's done for us.

There appears to be no term meaning "thank you"

in the Hebrew language. Many of our translations carry the word "thanks" or "thanksgiving," but these words are used in an explanatory sense. In the Old Testament culture the word used in place of "thanks" was "praise." The word often translated as "thanks" in the Old Testament is related to the word for "hand." The Hebrew concept of giving thanks is stretching out or lifting up of the hand to God.

In New Testament Greek, the word for "thanks" is the word *charis*. This is the root word from which "charismatic" comes from, and is related to the word for "grace." In other words, thanksgiving is an appropriate response to God's grace in our lives.

We must give thanks

The Word states in 1 Thessalonians 5:16-19:

16 Rejoice evermore.
17 Pray without ceasing.
18 In every thing give thanks: for this is the will of God in Christ Jesus concerning you.
19 Quench not the Spirit.

This is God's will for us. If we don't give thanks, we are out of God's will. There has been much confusion concerning this verse. Many people attribute everything that happens in their lives to God and they regard it as God's will for them.

But this poses a serious question. Are we supposed to give thanks when a friend is killed? When someone dies of cancer? At face value it appears that that is what this verse is saying. Some people do believe erroneously that everything that happens, good or bad, comes from God. If that is true, then I am supposed to thank God when an acquaintance of mine dies and goes to hell! This cannot be true.

The Bible in 1 John 3:8b declares, "For this purpose

the Son of God was manifested, that he might destroy the works of the Devil." If Jesus came to destroy the works of the Devil, then the Devil obviously has been working. How does he work? Jesus described the Devil's work in John 10:10, "The thief cometh not, but for to steal, and to kill, and to destroy: I am come that they might have life, and that they might have it more abundantly." The works of the Devil are stealing, killing, and destroying.

The Bible does not command us to thank God for the Devil's work. We are rather encouraged to thank God for what God has done. We must stop blaming God for the things that the Devil has been doing.

In 1 Thessalonians 5:18 we read, "In every thing give thanks: for this is the will of God in Christ Jesus concerning you." Notice the word "in." This is different than the word "for." We are not commanded to give thanks *for* everything that happens, we are to give thanks *in* the midst of whatever is happening.

We give thanks in the midst of disease by saying, "by his stripes we are healed" (1 Peter 2:24). I give thanks that He took my infirmities, and bare my sicknesses (Matthew 8:17). I give thanks according to Exodus 15:26 that, "I am the God that healeth thee." In other words, we give thanks for God's answer to Satan's attack. This is celebrating the triumph of Christ.

The simple principle is that we can give thanks for the Word of God. We don't give thanks for the things that have us bound; we give thanks that we don't have to remain bound. It is the Word of God that sets us free and our thanksgiving uplifts the power of that Word in our lives. This gets our faith moving and prepares us for the miracle working power of God.

Thanksgiving is a fruit of the Spirit

Thanksgiving essentially is an expression of the

fullness of the Holy Spirit. Ephesians 5:17-20 states:

17 **Wherefore be ye not unwise, but understanding what the will of the Lord is.**
18 **And be not drunk with wine, wherein is excess; but be filled with the Spirit;**
19 **Speaking to yourselves in psalms and hymns and spiritual songs, singing and making melody in your heart to the Lord;**
20 **Giving thanks always for all things unto God and the Father in the name of our Lord Jesus Christ.**

It is important that we notice what Paul is trying to say here. In verse 17 he commands us to understand the will of God, and then proceeds to tell us what the will of God is: to be filled with the Spirit and not to be drunk with wine. However, it is just as wrong for a Christian *not* to be filled with the Spirit, as it is for a Christian to be drunk with wine. In verse 19, Paul tells us how to fullfill the will of God by speaking to one another in psalms, hymns, and spiritual songs.

One of the manifestations of being filled with the Spirit is giving thanks to God. Thanksgiving is a manifestation of the infilling of the Holy Spirit. Don't claim to be filled with the Spirit if you are not a person who is constantly giving thanks unto the Lord. Matthew 12:34b says, "for out of the abundance of the heart the mouth speakth." If the heart is filled with thanksgiving, it will come out of our mouths.

We are to give thanks to God in the midst of all things. An unthankful person simply is not full of the Holy Spirit. The anointing of the Holy Spirit will continually manifest itself in thanksgiving that comes forth from our mouth. If we want to move into healing, if we want to see the manifestation of the power of God, then thanksgiving will release that anointing of the Holy

Spirit. As that thanksgiving comes out of our mouth, we prepare our inner man for what God will do in the Spirit.

Psalm 100:4-5 states that we are called to enter His gates with thanksgiving and to come into His courts with praise, to give thanks to Him. The first stage of our approach in coming before God involves thanksgiving. This gets us through the gate. In Psalm 100:5 we are told why we should thank the Lord: for He is good, His love and kindness is everlasting, His faithfulness is to all generations. We praise God not because of the way we feel, but because of who He is.

An important verse on thanksgiving is found in Philippians 4:6-7, "Be careful for nothing; but in every thing by prayer and supplication with thanksgiving let your request be made known unto God. And the peace of God, which passeth all understanding, shall keep your hearts and minds through Christ Jesus."

Notice the relationship here between supplication and thanksgiving. Supplication simply means to make a prayer request. Most of us regularly bring our requests to the Lord, asking Him to meet our various needs. Paul here makes it clear that *this kind of prayer must be preceded by thanksgiving.*

Thanksgiving must permeate all that we do, especially our praying. We are never to ask God for something without thanking Him first for what He has already done. This is the principle that prepares our heart for great faith. It is easy to see how, when we thank God for the great deeds of the past, we prepare out spirits to believe that, if He has done something like that in the past, he can also do something like that in the present. *Thanksgiving is a preliminary step to great faith.*

In fact, if we were to make a list of the recent events in our lives for which we can thank the Lord, and were to enumerate these before Him in our prayers, we would see far more answers to prayer than we do. It is impossible to go through a list of God's blessings without sensing a surge of faith in the inner man. This of course, prepares us for miracles of healing.

Thanksgiving strengthens faith

Thanksgiving has a way of getting the wheels of faith moving in our spirit. There is a certain amount of inertia in our faith that has to be overcome. Thanksgiving is action that we can take against that inertia to get our faith active. When we begin to recount what God has done, it doesn't take very long to get excited about what He is about to do now.

I am certain that the Devil hates thanksgiving. The power of thanksgiving through our personal testimony is more than we can imagine. Paul related his testimony of what God had done in his life several times in the New Testament. He was obsessed with God's intervention on his behalf.

Thanksgiving helps us to focus not on the problem, but on the answer. It reminds us that we are really victors when we are exalting God. The Devil will try to hold our minds by having us focus on the reality of the present. He will encourage us to think thoughts full of fear, but thanksgiving turns that whole process around and gets us moving in God's direction. I have noticed this principle over the years in the preaching of many men that God is using.

Thanksgiving is necessary to get faith moving strong. Notice in Philippians 4:6, Paul says, "in every thing by prayer and supplication with thanksgiving." This was not just a teaching of Paul, it was something that he did regularly.

All of Paul's prayers on behalf of believers began with thanks. In Romans 1:8 he says, "First, I thank my God through Jesus Christ for you all"; in Ephesians 1:15 he writes, "I cease not to give thanks for you"; Philippians 1:3, "I thank my God upon every remembrance of you"; Colossians 1:3, "We give thanks to God and the Father of our Lord Jesus Christ, praying always for you"; 1 Thessalonians 1:2, "We give thanks to God always for you all"; 2 Timothy 1:3, "thank God." Paul always thanked God first before he interceded for the people who were receiving his letter.

Thanksgiving also was important in the life of Jesus Christ. In John 6 we have the miraculous story of Jesus feeding the five thousand. A great multitude of people had been following him for quite some time. Jesus wanted to feed them and He told his disciples to find food.

Andrew found a little boy with five loaves and two fishes. He brought the food to Jesus, and Jesus took the loaves, and *after giving thanks,* He gave the food to the disciples to give to the people. He did not pray. He just gave thanks to the Father. His thanksgiving led to an immediate miracle that provided food enough to feed at least five thousand people.

Thanksgiving triggers miracles

Jesus did not perform this miracle as the Son of God. According to Acts 10:38 God anointed Jesus with the Holy Ghost and with power. It was the Holy Spirit working through Jesus that performed this miracle, and it was thanksgiving that triggered the ability of the Holy Spirit in Jesus for that miracle. *Thanksgiving therefore is the trigger that prepares us for the miracle-working power of God.*

In John 11, we have the story of Jesus raising Lazarus from the dead. When Jesus arrived in Bethany, the people were upset that He had not arrived earlier because they felt that He probably could have healed Lazarus before he died. Jesus was disturbed by their unbelief, and commanded that they roll the stone away from the door of the tomb.

When they took the stone away, Jesus lifted up his eyes, and said "Father, I thank thee that thou hast heard me." Notice the verb is past tense: "Father I thank You that You *have already heard* me." He simply gave thanks, and this thanksgiving was the trigger for the greatest miracle of his ministry. Lazarus rose from the dead when Jesus had given thanks.

There is no question that thanksgiving was manifested in the life of Jesus as a prelude to the manifestation of miracle-working power. In Luke 17, we have the story of ten lepers who came to Jesus for healing. He told them to go and show themselves to the priests, and as they went they were healed. Verse 15 says, "And one of them, when he saw that he was healed, turned back, and with a loud voice glorified God." He turned back and thanked God. And Jesus said to him, "Arise, go thy way: thy faith hath made thee whole."

Let us notice something about this story. All ten lepers were cleansed. They were all healed physically, but something extra happened to this one man. The phrase "thy faith hath made thee whole," is an interesting one. The word that Jesus used in the greek is *sozo* which means to save. It is an all inclusive word for salvation. It involves the salvation of the soul as well as the healing of the body. What Jesus is saying to the man is that his soul has been saved by his giving thanks to Jesus. *He was brought into a right eternal relationship with God by giving thanks for his healing.*

Giving thanks for what God has done in the past makes that deed permanent. If you have been healed and you want to remain healed, thank God continually for that healing. That makes it permanent. There is a great lesson to be learned here about the process of salvation as well. *Thanksgiving brings God's saving process into effect in our lives.* There is a great story from the Old Testament that further illlustrates the principle of thanksgiving. It is found in the book of Jonah.

It was a great sacrifice for Jonah to thank God in the midst of his situation, but it was thanksgiving that got his faith moving. It is very difficult for us to praise God in those kinds of circumstances. You may feel that you are in the belly of the fish. You may feel that there is seaweed tied around your neck and that you are about to die. But if you are willing to thank God in the circumstances no matter how bad it is, you get faith moving in your spirit and prepare yourself for a miracle from God.

2. The meaning and purpose of praise

The Psalms of David can be divided into two groups: Psalms of descriptive praise, and Psalms of declarative praise. In the Psalms of declarative praise, the emphasis is on what God has done for His people. These Psalms declare the glory of God. Thanksgiving relates directly to the Psalms of declarative praise. In the Psalms of descriptive praise the psalmist exults in the person of God, His attributes, in essence, who He is.

A relationship with God cannot exist without praise. There is no impersonal way of expressing praise to the Almighty. Of all the books in the Old Testament, the book of Psalms is the most read by the Christian family. Somehow we find expression to our inmost thoughts, to our moments of great joy, and to those times of terror when we seem to be cut off from Him. The Psalms have everything. Music, beauty, wisdom, theology and experience.

The English word "psalms" is a transliteration of the Greek title of the book. The Greek word *psalmoi* was first translated into Latin as *psalmi* and then into English as "psalms." The Greek literally meant, "a striking of the fingers on the string of a guitar, or a musical stringed instrument." Then the word took the extended meaning of "a song with string accompaniment." So the meaning of the Greek title of the book is "sacred songs sung to music accompaniment." The book of Psalms is a book of music. The Hebrew word for Psalm is *tehilim,* a term of music. The longest book in the Bible is a book of music.

Sometimes the Psalms express a lament, but even those Psalms finally end in praise. Praise according to *Webster's Third New International Dictionary* means, "the act of glorifying or extolling God."[1] Praise means speaking well of, extolling, or magnifying the virtues of someone. Praise comes from a close relationship with God. Praise must always be vocal. It is not silent. Thanksgiving occurs when we whisper a prayer of thanks to God. Praise occurs when we tell someone else about God's goodness.

Words of praise

The best way to understand what praise means is to examine the words used for praise in the Old Testament, and particularly in the Pslams. The first word for praise in the Hebrew is *halal.* We have this word in the English language in the transliteration "hallelujah." It means simply, praise the Lord, or "Praise Yah". Yah is the shortened form of the Old Testament Yahweh, translated in the King James as *Jehovah.*

The word *halal* means, to be boastful, to be excited, and to enjoy. This word connotes a tremendous explosion of enthusiasm in the act of praising. It is what a person does when their favorite sports team has won the victory in the last fifteen seconds of the game. If they are a real fan, they will stand, raise their hands in the air, and shout in victory. This is the essence of the meaning of the word *halal.*

Very few of us ever praise the Lord in this fashion. We are to boast of God's exploits and extol His greatness with such enthusiasm and excitement that others would think it foolish. The man who praises in this fashion is overwhelmed with the love that he feels for the Lord. He is not acting foolishly before the Lord. It is just those around him that think he is. That is the meaning of the word *halal.*

The next word is *yadah,* and means to acknowledge in public, as in Psalm 138:1, "I will give Thee thanks with all my heart; I will sing praises to Thee before the gods" (NASB). A better translation of the verb to thank or praise, is to give public aknowledgement to. This word expresses the core meaning of praise. It is telling others what God has done. This verb has a root meaning of "the extended hand," or, "to throw out the hand." It implies worshipping with raised hands.

This is the word used in 2 Chronicles 20:19-21, where the Levites go out before the army praising the Lord. The word for praise in the Hebrew is *yadah.* As they went they lifted their hands with all their might. They expressed their praise unto God with their uplifted hands, and of course, we know what happened; the enemy self-destructed.

Our hands express so much of our personality. We can make a fist and strike someone. We can reach out and touch someone with our hands to bless them. Or, we can raise our hands in praise to God. Psalm 63:4 says, "Thus will I bless thee while I live: I will lift up my hands in thy name."

Another word in the Hebrew is *barak*. The word *barak* means simply to bless. It is one of the most interesting words for praise in the Old Testament. We have all been blessed by God. He has given us the gift of eternal life. He has healed our bodies. He has blessed us with families and with financial supply.

We are blessed, but the question comes, How can we bless God? Psalm 103:1-2 says, "Bless the Lord, O my soul: and all that is within me, bless his holy name. Bless the Lord, O my soul, and forget not all [or any of] his benefits." We bless the Lord by not forgetting Him, and not forgetting His blessing. Psalm 103 then goes on to enumerate those blessings: lovingkindness, satisfaction, redemption, honor, renewal. We bless the Lord by remembering all of these things.

There is a sense of kneeling and blessing God as an act of adoration in the word *barak*. There is a reflex reaction in all of us that wants to bow in the presence of the Lord, especially in prayer. In Psalm 72:9-15, God promises to set the poor and the afflicted free if they will bow before Him and by the act of bowing expect to receive His blessings. The concept here is a very simple, if we will kneel before Him and stay there expecting to receive His promises we shall receive.

The next word for praise is *zamar*. This is one of the musical verbs for praise in the book of Psalms. It carries the idea of making music in praise to God as in Psalm 92:1, "It is a good thing to give thanks unto the Lord [public acknowledgement to Jehovah], and to sing praises unto thy name, O most High." It is impossible to understand praise without understanding its relationship to music.

Music was the foremost expression of praise by God's children in the Old Testament. It is impossible to have vocal, extended praise for any period of time without music being involved. The word *zamar* means to touch the strings, and refers to praise that involves instrumental worship as delineated in Psalm 150.

The next word for praise is *shabach.* This word is found in Psalm 117:1, "O Praise the Lord, all ye nations: praise him, all ye people." The word praise in this context means to laud, to speak well of in a high and befitting way. *Shabach* also means to address in a loud tone, to command triumph, glory, to shout. In Psalm 63:3-4 David says, "Because thy lovingkindness is better than life, my lips shall praise thee [shabach]. Thus will I bless thee while I live." There is a time when it is appropriate to give a loud shout unto the Lord. This is the *shabach.* This is the kind of praise that makes the Devil shut up.

The next Hebrew word for praise is *towdah.* It is related to the word *yadah.* In the "New American Standard Bible", it is translated as thanksgiving. It also involves the extension of the hand in adoration. It is used in the book of Psalms to thank God for things that have not yet happened, as well as for those things already completed. Psalm 50:23, "Whoso offereth praise glorifieth me: and to him that ordereth his conversation aright will I shew the salvation of God." The word for praise here is *towdah,* and it has the distinct connotation of sacrifice.

Towdah is directly related to the concept of sacrifice as it relates to praise. If we are willing to sacrifice praise now, then we shall see a manifestation of the salvation of God. We praise Him before the event. The sacrifice of praise as an act of faith is implicit in the word *towdah,* especially as it is used in this verse.

Towdah then is a sacrifice of praise, rejoicing in something that is promised in the Word but which has not yet taken place. There is great spiritual power in the use of the Word this way. This is what happens in my praise and healing rallies when I encourage people to praise the Lord before there has been any manifestation of healing from God.

As people raise their hearts and hands in praise to the Lord, it involves a sacrifice, especially if they are very sick in their bodies. The carnal mind would fight at this point and ridicule this particular action. But there is great faith in *towdah* as praise. It is the sacrifice that God honors by His performing of miracles.

Tehillah is another Hebrew word meaning to sing, to laud. *Tehillah* is singing our halals. It is used in Psalm 22:3 where we read that God inhabits (sits enthroned on) the praises of His people. God manifests Himself in the midst of exuberant singing.

In 2 Chronicles 20:22, when Israel began to sing and to praise, God set ambushments. This refers to a special kind of singing. It is singing unprepared, unrehearsed songs; probably what we would know today as "singing in the spirit." This expression of praise brings tremendous unity to the body of Christ. Other references to *tehillah* are found in Psalms 34:1, Psalms 40:3 and Psalms 66:2.

Another Hebrew word for praise is *ruah.* This word means to shout in joy. In the Old Testament, a believer had no problem with getting very excited about the reality of his relationship with God as expressed in Psalm 95:1, "let us make a joyful noise to the rock of our salvation," and Psalm 100:1, "Make a joyful noise unto the

Lord, all ye lands." There is a certain authenticity, genuineness, and intensity expressed by this verb that demands verbal expression.

There are many other words that also relate to praise in the Psalms. One word is *qara:* Psalm 116:17, "I will offer to thee the sacrifice of thanksgiving, and will call upon the name of the Lord." The idea there is proclamation, announcing and proclaiming the name of the Lord. Another verb is ***nagad*** meaning to declare. Another related word is ***basar*** which means to proclaim. Another Hebrew word is *rum* meaning to extol.

The important thing to notice about all these verbs for praise in the Old Testament is that they are words of sound. Praise in the Old Testament always is accompanied with sound. It is vocal, it is public, and it is excited.

An examination of the Psalms makes it clear that praise must be a strong emphasis of our church services today. We must be afforded the opportunity to minister to each other in praise. We need to use our lips to glorify His name. Thanksgiving relates more to what God has done, while praise relates to who God is. This distinction is not absolute, but it is a good guide.

3. The meaning and purpose of worship

The English word worship comes from the Old English word "weordhscipe." This word was later shortened to "worthship." It still is used in English law when the judge is referred to as "your worship." Worship in the verb form means to pay homage or respect. There also are many synonyms that help us understand the meaning of the word. Words such as adore, esteem, magnify, revere, venerate, exalt.

The Hebrew word for worship in the Old Testament is *shachah.* It is translated, to bow down, to do reverence, to prostrate, beseech humbly. *It is impossible to understand worship without relating it to an attitude of the body.* Sometimes it refers to a stretching out of the hands towards God. Sometimes a bending of the knee. In Leviticus 9:24, the people fell face down before the power of the Lord.

The most commonly used word for worship in the New Testament is *proskuneo.* This word is used over fifty times. It is a combination of two separate Greek words *pros* which means towards, and *kuneo* which means to kiss. *Proskuneo* literally means to kiss towards. The meaning of the word is perfectly expressed by the woman who washed the feet of Jesus with her tears and then kissed His feet.

Man is made to worship

Man is essentially a worshipping creature. It is part of his nature. His choice is not whether he will worship, but only whom he will worship. In the Scriptures God demands his worship. He will not share our worship with anyone or anything else.

When the Devil tried to tempt Jesus in the wilderness and said, "All these kingdoms of the world will I give you if you bow down and worship me," Jesus responded to him, "Get thee hence, Satan: for it is written, Thou shalt worship the Lord thy God, and him only shalt thou serve (Mat. 4:10)."

This illustrates a great principle of worship. Whatever we worship we ultimately will end up serving. The more we worship something or someone, the more our commitment increases, and the more we become like the thing we worship.

Worship is the ultimate decision. We cannot

change our nature. *Our nature demands that we worship something. Our choice is whether it will be God or something else.* Traditionally down through the centuries man has worshipped many things other than God. He has worshipped wooden idols, he has worshipped his physical desires, he has worshipped money and possessions, he has worshipped political leaders, he has worshipped false religion.

Of course, all false worship is dictated and controlled by Satan. So in essence when we worship the wrong things, we literally are worshipping the Devil.

In the story of the woman at the well, in John 4, we have a classic story of worship. Jesus was traveling with His disciples on His way to Galilee. The road led them through a town in Samaria. They arrived at Jacob's well outside the town where Jesus sat down to rest, while the disciples went into the city to find food. Jesus was surprised to see a woman coming to draw water in the hot afternoon. All the other women in the city drew their water in the early morning. Jesus entered into a conversation with the woman.

It turned out that she had had five husbands, and the man she was currently living with was not her husband. There obviously was a deep craving in her spirit. Jesus knew that immorality would not quench that craving. The craving of her spirit actually was a craving after God, a craving for worship. So Jesus led the conversation to the subject of worship.

Jesus knew it would not be enough to rebuke the woman for her immoral conduct. He had to satisfy the need that existed in her spirit, and so He said to her, in John 4:23, "But the hour cometh, and now is, when the true worshippers shall worship the Father in spirit and in truth: for the Father seeketh such to worship him."

It is an exciting, even an amazing fact, that *God is seeking for people to worship Him.* The very fact that God can be worshipped provides an incredible opportunity for each one of us. The fact that the great God of the universe would take note of the worship of humble creatures, is hard to comprehend.

Worship in spirit and truth

Notice the phrase "in spirit and in truth." "In truth" means absolute openness and honesty before God, hiding nothing. It involves exposing our entire life to the divine searchlight of His Holy Spirit. "In spirit" refers to a part of the total human personality.

In 1 Thessalonians 5:23, the Scripture refers to man as a three dimensional being. He is composed of spirit, soul, and body. Man's body relates to the world around him through the five senses. His body is world-conscious. The soul of man is self-conscious. The spirit of man is God-conscious. God is a spirit, and they that worship Him must worship Him in spirit and in truth.

The only way to worship then is through the spirit. It is not the soul or the body that worships, but the spirit.

Those who truly worship are those who flow toward God in their spirit, but do so according to the truth of God's Word. Paul says in Ephesians 5:18, "And be not drunk with wine, wherein is excess; but be filled with the Spirit." Being filled with the Spirit inevitably has to involve worship. That craving within the spirit of man can drive one man to drink while it drives another man to God.

When Jesus confronted the woman at the well, she did everything she could to avoid the point of the discussion. She tried to sidetrack the conversation by discussing the race issue between the Jews and the

Samaritans. Jesus brought her back to the subject of worship. She went on to discuss the origin of the well, and how the well had come to them from Jacob, Jesus brought her back to worship.

As He talked about the water of life, she thought He meant physical water and requested some to meet her natural needs. Jesus confronted her on the isse of her husband. Finally, she tried to sidetrack the conversation again by discussing the prophetic issue. Jesus again brought her back to worship.

This is a classic study for all of us. Some of us would discuss race, others of us would discuss church buildings, others among us would discuss natural needs, or prophetic office. We would do anything we can to sidestep the issue of worship.

Jesus confronted the woman with this statement, "The hour cometh, and now is, when the true worshippers shall worship the Father in spirit and in truth: for the Father seeketh such to worship him." The hour to worship God is *now.* Not tomorrow or yesterday, but *now.* We don't need to wait until Sunday. We don't need to wait until we sit in our pew in church. God is available to us at all times.

It is very difficult to describe what worship really is. It is much easier to describe what worship does. Worship can bow, kneel, we can lay prostrate on our faces in worship, but yet it is not the bowing, the kneeling or the prostration that makes worship what it is.

Worship is a response to a relationship with God, but that relationship is very intimate and it is very difficult for another person to describe exactly what it is. It does involve fellowship. It does involve personal revelation by God to the individual. But it basically is the outpouring of inner thoughts to God, often accompanied by emotional and expressive actions of the body. But we always must remember that it is almost impossible to describe in words the inner sense and feeling that permeates the relationship. As the old Scotsman said, "It is better felt than telt."

Moving into God's presence

Thanksgiving, praise and worship should be compared to the three areas of the tabernacle of Moses. The outer court represents thanksgiving; the holy place represents praise; and the Holy of Holies represents worship.

According to Psalm 110, we enter His gates with thanksgiving. Thanksgiving relates to what God has done. As we come to the outer court of the temple preparing ourself to come into the Holy of Holies, we begin with a recounting of what the Lord has done. This involves much action of the body. It involves the raising of the hands. Perhaps the clapping of the hands, a loud voice, excitement, and the exuberance that marks the beginning of our approach to the Lord.

We move then to the holy place where we offer up praise. Praise is a function of the will which is represented by the table of showbread in the holy place. It also flows out of an enlightened mind which is represented by the golden candlestick. A mind set on fire by the Holy Spirit, enlightened by the power of the prayer language. Praise like that becomes as a sweet smelling fragrance or incense from off the golden altar of incense which represents our emotion.

First we will to praise God, then we sanctify our minds through the power of the Spirit, then our emotions take over and bring us through the veil into the presence of God in worship. When we come to that final act of worship it is the divine invitation of the Lord

Himself that draws us within the veil.

No man can program himself for worship. It is an act of the will to thank God, it is an act of the will to praise God. *It is an act of God's will to invite us into His presence in the act of worship* and it is only when our relationship with God is consumated in worship that we truly feel that we are where He is and He is where we are.

[1] *Webster's Third New International Dictionary Unabridged*, s.v. "praise."

9

Principles Of Praise

Praise silences the Devil

This is one of the most important facts for practical Christian living. Every believer needs to learn how to make the Devil shut up. Praise is the way to silence him. Praise will stop the oppression of his evil thoughts. Praise will bring the weapons of God to bear against the attack of the Evil One.

Psalms 8:1,2 declares:

1 O Lord our Lord, how excellent is thy name in all the earth! who hast set thy glory above the heavens.
2 Out of the mouth of babes and sucklings hast thou ordained strength because of thine enemies, that thou mightest still the enemy and the avenger.

Several points need to be made about these two Scripture verses. In verse 1, David says "how excellent is thy name in all the earth." Notice the weapon that David is using here is the Name of the Lord. The launching vehicle or rocket that sends forth the Name against strongholds is the launching rocket of praise.

So as we begin to read the Psalms, we immediately begin to recognize that David is launching into spiritual warfare. Then he says, "out of the mouth of babes and sucklings hast thou ordained strength because of thine enemies." Notice "enemies" here is used in the plural. I believe he is refering directly to evil spirits, the instruments that Satan uses to come against the believer. Everyone of us is under attack from evil spirits.

Notice the next phrase, "that thou mightest still the enemy and the avenger." David here speaks of the enemy in the singular. He is referring directly to Satan.

Because of Satan and his many demon spirits coming against believers, God has ordained a method for believers to make them be silent. This verse says "that thou mightest still." A practical translation of that would be, "that You might make the Devil shut up." There is tremendous strength here in the ability of the believer to make the Devil shut up, and the way he does this is "out of the mouths of babes and sucklings."

We have an interesting cross-reference to this verse in Matthew 21:16. It is the time of the triumphal entry into Jerusalem. The people have welcomed Jesus as He comes from the Mount of Olives. He is riding on a donkey colt. A great multitude have spread their garments in the way and others have cut down branches from the trees. Everyone is crying "Hosanna to the Son of David." As He comes into the city, He goes to the temple and casts out the moneychangers, but the children have continued with Him and they are making much noise.

Matthew 21:15 indicates that the chief priests and the scribes were very upset when they saw the children praising Him this way, and they came to Jesus and said, "Don't You hear what they're saying?" Jesus replied to them with a quote from Psalms 8:2, but He changes the words that David wrote. He says in His reply, "Yea; have ye never read, Out of the mouth of babes and sucklings thou hast perfected praise?" It is interesting to compare the two verses. In the King James Version, David said, "out of the mouth of babes and sucklings hast though ordained strength." Jesus says, "hast thou perfected praise."

This is a very simple and yet direct teaching of Jesus. Because Jesus is the Word of God He has the right to interpret Scripture. He did not *misquote* David. He rather *interpreted* what David had been trying to say.

Our power in dealing with the Devil; the ordained strength of God that goes into effect on our behalf, happens when we move into praise. *Praise is the ordained strength of God.* But we must become as simple as a child to do it. Jesus said concerning His disciples at one point, "Father I thank thee that you have hid these things from the wise and hast revealed them unto babes."

Paul says, "as newborn babes, desire the sincere milk of the word that you may grow thereby." Most of us are like spiritual babies. We seem to be easy prey for the Devil. How do we silence the Devil? The ordained strength of God's people in battle is their perfected praise. The weaker we are as babes and sucklings, the more God is glorified.

Praise comes from the mouth

Notice the use of the word "mouth" in this verse. All spiritual weapons have only one launching pad, and that is the mouth. The mouth is the center of all spiritual warfare and here the weapons of God are launched out of the mouth of babes and sucklings.

In Revelation 16:13 Scripture says, "And I saw three unclean spirits like frogs come out of the mouth of the dragon, and out of the mouth of the beast, and out of the mouth of the false prophet." The mouth can launch the Devil's weapons in the same way that it can launch God's weapons. All spiritual weapons are launched through the mouth.

There is a very important lesson here. Our mouths must be watched over, because no matter what we say with our mouths, we are launching weapons of one sort or another. Those weapons must be God's weapons and not the Devil's. If we don't use our mouths correctly, we simply make it impossible for us to win the battle.

What comes out of our mouth ultimately settles the conflict with the Evil One, and that is why the challenge of praise is so important for the believer. God has ordained that the believer exercise this kind of strength and it has one primary effect: It makes the Devil shut up. Our mind cannot be invaded with his thoughts. Our mouths cannot be polluted with his words.

It is important in a situation where deliverance is to be ministered to people that an atmosphere of praise be created. I have been in services when we moved into an atmosphere of high praise where the evil spirits that were oppressing people in the room began to cry out. Praise so upset them, that it demanded a response on their part. This simply revealed who they were and who they were holding authority over and a word of deliverance set the people free.

It is so important that we watch what comes out of our mouths. Our mouths are the way we cast our vote. When we praise the Lord, we are casting our vote for God and against the Devil. This moves us into a tremendous place of spiritual victory.

Praise is a garment of the Spirit

Isaiah 61:3 speaks of "the garment of praise for the spirit of heaviness." Isaiah 61 was quoted by Jesus in his home synagogue in Nazareth immediately after His temptation in the wilderness. He was invited by the Rabbi to read the Scripture and He read the words of Isaiah. Then He stated that, "today is this scripture fulfilled in your ears." So it is obvious that we are dealing with a prophetic portion of Scripture here.

In verse 3 of Isaiah 61, we have a continuation of the preaching of the good tidings. This is what God has sent Christ and all believers to minister with. God gives beauty for ashes, He gives the oil of joy for mourning, He gives the garment of praise for the spirit of heaviness.

This is the three-fold exchange of the Gospel. When we preach the Gospel of Christ to someone, we give them beauty for their sadness and ashes. The Gospel is the oil of joy for a mourning spirit. Oil here represents the Holy Spirit. We also have a garment of praise for the spirit of heaviness.

There are many people in contemporary society wrestling against the spirit of heaviness. This spirit is more than just heaviness. In contemporary language we would call it a spirit of depression. It is more than just an influence. It is an actual principality, a stronghold of the Devil. It is an evil personality, a spirit that grips the hearts and minds of people as they look at the negative side of life. It is a spirit that binds, that discourages, that frustrates. It is not merely an attitude, but an actual evil spirit.

How do we get free of this spiritual bondage? In my travels I have noticed this is one of the most common spirits that binds people. Praise is a spiritual garment and every believer must wear this garment at all times. But it is something we must put on. We literally have to clothe ourselves with this garment. This again refers directly to the act of the will in praising God.

When we get out of bed each morning we decide what clothes we will wear. We walk to the closet and make a distinct decision. In the same way, we must decide to put on the garment of praise when we come against the spirit of depression that would bind everyone of us.

You see our praise creates an atmosphere that actually embarrasses Satan because he desires our worship. The most compelling drive of his nature is to receive worship of men. When we determine that we are going to give that worship to God, nothing makes him angrier, nothing embarrasses him more. He must go somewhere else when we create an atmosphere of praise. We trouble him much more than he can trouble us. It is very important that we be aware of that.

Praise leads the believer into the triumph of Christ

Psalms 106:47 states, "Save us, O Lord our God, and gather us from among the heathen, to give thanks unto thy holy name, and to triumph in thy praise." This verse applies not only to Israel as a nation, but also to the Church itself. *We are to triumph in the praise of God.*

There is a great difference between victory and triumph. *Victory is the accomplishment of the defeat of the enemy.* It is the winning of the battle, the silencing of the Devil. *Triumph* involves much more than victory. Victory makes a triumph possible, but *a triumph is a celebration of the victory already won.*

Colossians 2:15 states, "And having spoiled principalities and powers, he made a shew of them openly, triumphing over them in it." This is what God did for us in Christ Jesus. The verse refers to principalities and powers. In an earlier chapter, I described them as fallen princes, operative with various levels of authority in Satan's kingdom.

This verse says that Jesus spoiled these principalities and powers. It means He made their power of no effect. He stripped them of their authority. Through the cross of Jesus Christ, God stripped Satan of all his powers and Jesus triumphed over Satan.

Notice 2 Corinthians 2:14 in this regard: "Now thanks be unto God, which always causeth us to triumph in Christ, and maketh manifest the savour of his knowledge by us in every place." This triumph that Jesus accomplished by stripping Satan of all his powers has been transferred by Christ to the Church.

When we come into Christ we are brought into IIis triumph. Notice the adverbial phrases of the verse. There is no time and no place when God does *not* cause us to triumph. God always causes us to triumph in Christ. A modern translation has it this way, "it makes us a continuing pageant of triumph in Christ."

It's important to notice again the distinction between victory and triumph. Jesus won the victory on the cross. *He does not ask us to win the victory.* The old idea of preachers admonishing the saints to win the victory is not scripturally based. You can't win a victory that has already been won. We have, however, been invited to share the triumph, and this is a very important distinction. We can share the triumph of Christ. God always causes us to triumph in Christ.

When Paul uses the term triumph, he is referring to a Roman custom. William Shakespeare was acquainted with the Roman custom. In his play, *Julius Caesar*, it is in the midst of a Roman triumph that Cassius and Brutus conspire to kill Julius Caesar.

Remember, a triumph was the highest honor that could be bestowed upon any successful Roman general. If he had done exploits for the Roman empire; if he had been successful in his battle; if he had defeated his enemies in an outstanding manner; when he returned to Rome the Senate would vote him a triumph. Remember, a triumph was a celebration of victory.

There was a special kind of organization for the triumph. The general was placed in a special triumphal chariot pulled by two horses, and was led through the streets of Rome. That particular day was declared a holiday in the city and the people of Rome would line the streets and applaud for the general when he passed.

Behind the chariot were brought evidences of the general's victories. The rulers of the conquered nations were lined up as prisoners of war and led in chains behind the chariot. Rank after rank came the defeated army generals, captains, majors, lieutenants. Even wild beasts indigenous to the conquered country. The idea was to create visible evidence of what the man had won.

Paul uses the triumph analogy to make vivid our victory. What he says in Colossians 2:15 is that Satan and all his forces, principalities, powers, the rulers of the darkness of this world, spiritual wickedness in the heavenlies; all those forces are being led behind the chariot of Jesus as evidence of their defeat. They have been stripped of their armor. They have been spoiled. Now Paul in 2 Corinthians 2:14 says God always causes us to triumph in Christ. God causes us to join the pageant of triumph with Christ.

In order to do this, we must accept a certain mindset. We do not pray to God *to give* us the victory. *Our praise makes us a part of the victory celebration. We triumph in our praise.* The battle already is won, *past tense.* Our praise ties us into a celebration of the victory that has been won.

Our triumphant praise begins to relate healing effectively to our bodies. When we thank God that His finished work also relates to our financial needs, we celebrate the fact that in Christ we are victorious over financial problems. This is true in our interpersonal relationships between husband and wife, parents and children.

The triumph directly relates to our praise. Our praise moves us into a position of triumph. *We're not fighting the battle when we praise, we're praising God that the battle already has been won. This is a key.*

We're in the chariot with Jesus. How do we get into the chariot? We get into the chariot when we celebrate His victory. Praise is celebration of victory. When we open our church services to a celebration of victory; the fact that disease is defeated, the fact that financial oppression is defeated; the fact that demonic oppression is defeated; the fact that we are set free and will be set free as we triumph; praise then becomes a tremendous release to the believer's faith.

When we praise Him for what He has done on our behalf, we literally step into the chariot. We take our place with Christ. We stop crying and fretting and begging and pleading. We change the order of our faith and our faith begins to celebrate. It begins to say, "I have been healed 2,000 years ago in Christ." Praise the Lord !

Praise brings revelation

Revelation comes through praise. Psalms 49:4 says,

"I will incline mine ear to a parable: I will open my dark saying upon the harp." When the prophetic anointing came upon David, he often uttered "dark sayings." Things which he himself did not readily understand. This often happens when the spirit of prophecy comes upon someone during praise. There may be things uttered that are not easily understood. As David played his harp, as he sang and praised the Lord, the Scripture indicates that the dark sayings were opened.

It's interesting to notice the connection here between the spirit of the prophet and the musician. Often prophets were also musicians in Old Testament times, and I think this relates to the New Testament church as well.

But there was something about the act of praise and music that opened David's heart to the reception of revelation from God. He entered into worship and God responded with revelation. So praise became a means by which the Word of God was opened to David. The prophetic anointing was explained. In the same way today, the Scriptures are opened to God's people through praise and worship.

Praise prepares you to understand the subtle meanings of God's Word. It prepares you for the *rhema* revelation of the Word of God. When we find portions of the Word of God which are difficult for us to understand and we enter into praise contemplating that particular Scripture, one of the facts of praise is that we can expect to come into that place in the presence of God whereby His Holy Spirit will shed His light upon the dark sayings. He will open His Word for His people. Praise directly relates to the revelation of the *rhema* word of God.

Praise and worship prepare our hearts for the reception of the *rhema.* They prepare the human spirit to hear what God is trying to communicate to us. It is interesting to note in this regard in Matthew 4:4 Jesus' response to the Devil to turn the stones into bread. He said "Man shall not live by bread alone, but by every word [rhema] that proceedeth [is now proceeding] out of the mouth of God."

There is a *now* Word of God coming to each one of us. A *now* revelation of the Holy Spirit, directly related to our circumstances. Praise opens us and prepares us for the reception of that *rhema* Word of God and this in turn brings great revelation from the Holy Spirit to our hearts.

Praise prepares us for miracles

When the Devil comes against us, praise will always point a way out. Psalms 50:23 says, "Whoso offereth [sacrifices] praise glorifieth me: and to him that ordereth his conversation [way of life] aright will I shew the salvation of God."

The word for salvation here in the Old Testament, as well as the word for salvation in the New Testament, refers to more than just the salvation of the soul. It refers to divine healing. It refers to the many ways in which God helps us. It also refers directly to deliverance from satanic attack. This verse indicates that when we sacrifice praise and glorify God, that He will show us His salvation. He will come to us and deliver us. He will set us free.

When we offer praise to God, we should look for a demonstration of His salvation and deliverance. When we praise God, we prepare a way for Him to intervene. Two classic examples of this fact of praise can be found in Jonah, and Paul and Silas.

The story of Jonah is outlined for us in his book. The facts are fairly simple. God called Jonah to minister His Gospel to the people of Nineveh. Jonah did not like the Ninevites and tried to run away from the call of God on his life. The Bible says he went down to Tarshish and there he caught a ship, and endeavored to escape from what God was calling him to.

Immediately, as the ship set sail, a great violent storm came upon them. It seemed as though the ship was on it's way to the bottom. The sailors came to Jonah after they had cast lots and the lot fell to Jonah. They said to him, "What is the reason for this evil coming upon us? What have you done wrong?" He told them that he was a Hebrew and was running from God. The sailors were afraid and decided to cast him into the sea.

The Bible says that the Lord had prepared a great fish to swallow Jonah, and Jonah was in the belly of the fish three days and three nights. It is hardly possible for us to imagine the kind of situation he was in. There was seaweed wrapped around his neck, the digestive juices of the fish were eating at his flesh. It was a very uncomfortable situation.

In chapter two, the Bible outlines a prayer that Jonah prayed out of the fish's belly. He complains about the water compassing him about and the weeds wrapped around his neck. However, in verse nine he seems to hit a spiritual hot button. For eight verses his prayer has been that of complaint. Then he says, "But I will sacrifice unto thee with the voice of thanksgiving; I will pay that that I have vowed. Salvation is of the Lord." In the next verse, the Bible says that, "the Lord spake unto the fish, and it vomitted out Jonah upon the dry land."

Something about Jonah's prayer lined him up for

deliverance. When Jonah offered God thanksgiving, the fish couldn't hold him down any longer. The moral of this story is obvious: When we are down in the "belly of the fish," when it seems that everyone has forgotten us, when it's difficult to do anything, all we can do is pray. In our prayer we must stay away from complaining and offer a sacrifice of thanksgiving and praise to the Lord. When we do this obediently, then God speaks to the source of our complaint and we find deliverance.

Another illustration of praise as a way to deliverance is found in the story of Paul and Silas in the Philippian jail. After great persecution by the inhabitants of Phillipi and after being beaten, Paul and Silas were cast into prison. Acts 16:25 declares what they did, "And at midnight Paul and Silas prayed, and sang praises unto God."

Imagine what they could have been saying to God that night. They could have complained. They could have listed all the problems that had come about because of their missionary journeys. They could have asked the Lord to put them in a different line of employment. But they prayed and sang praises unto God.

They didn't do it quietly. The Bible records, "and the prisoners heard them." They were singing out loud. The Greek in that phrase implies that the prisoners were listening keenly. They must have been surprised at praise coming from prisoners who had been beaten so badly. They probably thought that those two missionaries were crazy.

Acts 16:26 states, "And suddenly there was a great earthquake, so that the foundations of the prison were shaken: and immediately all the doors were opened, and every one's bands were loosed." This illustrates the fact that God responds to praise. Praise is a way to bring

God into your situation. Praise is a way to bring the miracle working power of God into your life.

But notice again that it has to be a sacrifice. It is the abnormal thing to do. If things are going well, it is never a sacrifice to praise the Lord. But God delights when you offer a *sacrifice* of praise to Him. It is a tremendous step of faith and God honors that faith with miracles.

God inhabits our praises

Psalms 22:3 declares, "But Thou art holy, O thou that inhabitest the praises of Israel." God lives in the midst of the praises of His people. The word "inhabitest" in the Hebrew means to actually sit or reside in a place. The Swedish have an excellent alternate in their translation of that verse; it says, "Thou are enthroned upon the praises of Israel."

God is always king whether we praise Him or not. He is worthy of praise whether He receives that praise or not. But when we praise Him we offer Him a throne to sit upon in *our* presence. That is why our praise is so necessary in order *to bring the power of the presence of God into our church services.*

When we join together to praise Him, aside from the practical value that the praise creates in the hearts of the people, we literally offer a throne to the King. When we offer Him that kind of throne, we can be assured He will come and occupy that throne. He literally will inhabit our praises. Praise is the throne that the King of Kings sits upon, and He sits upon that throne in the midst of us.

The opposite also is true. If we don't praise, we're withholding a throne from the King. That is why any church service without praise is literally pointless. If we go to church to enter the presence of God and we do not create a throne for Him to sit upon with our praise, then the service is null and void. It does no good. The throne has not been provided, so the King is not present.

Obviously Scripture says that, "where two or three of us are gathered together in His name, He shall be in the midst." However, notice it says *in His name.* There must be a unity in the name, and that unity comes in the midst of praise. Praise creates unity in the hearts of the believers and provides a throne for the King to sit upon.

God is a holy God, He cannot and will not inhabit an unholy atmosphere. Often the atmosphere will be tainted and corrupted with impure speech and impure thoughts. When we all enter into praise, praise literally sanctifies the atmosphere. It changes our thoughts from the negative to the thoughts of God.

When we begin to extol the mighty deeds that He has done, to magnify His name and who He is, we begin to think God's thoughts. As we do, the polluted atmosphere of our minds, and the strongholds that move in supernatural areas around us, are transformed by the act of praise.

Praise is the way into God's presence

When Christians begin to pray, they often feel far off from God, that God is distant. They can be absolutely correct in their doctrine and have a good grasp of Scripture, but they have no sense of fellowship with God. They don't really know Him intimately.

Everyone of us has a fundamental drive and desire for access to God's presence. We may be afraid of Him, but all of us have a desire to be in His presence. The Scripture is very clear in telling us that praise is the only avenue of access to God. Psalms 100:4 states, "Enter into His gates with thanksgiving, and into His courts with praise: be thankful unto him, and bless His name."

The way through the gate is thanksgiving; the way into the court is praise. If we want to enter, there is no other way. We must come through the avenue of praise. Praise and singing is the protocol in coming before the King. The psalmist writes, "come before His presence with singing."

The protocol of praise

In 1974, the Lord strongly impressed me during a concert in a Roman Catholic church in Tampa, Florida, that He was going to lead us to minister among Roman Catholic people worldwide. I fought against that initial leading. I had the traditional Protestant hang-ups about Roman Catholics, but I could not escape from the call of God to minister to these people.

Three months later we were in St. Anne's Cathedral in downtown Warsaw, Poland. During our first concert in the church, out of an audience of 2,500 people, 350 responded to accept the claims of the Lordship of Christ on their lives.

Three days later the Cardinal primate of the nation, Stephan Cardinal Wyzchinski, invited us to sing in all of their major cathedrals. He informed me that the Communist government thoroughly controlled the school systems and they were telling the students that God was dead. But he said they would listen to our music and praise.

He opened the churches of the nation to us. The next year, 1975, we ministered to a huge crowd of over 100,000 people at the famous festival of the Black Madonna in Czestochowa, Poland. Again, in 1976, we sang at the same festival with approximately a quarter of a million people in attendance. Also in attendance at that festival was a cardinal from the south of Poland, named Karol Cardinal Wojtyla. He listened to us sing and preach and later invited us into his home for fellowship. He loved young people, he loved our music.

When the leader of our team, Joel Vesanen, asked him to write us a letter of recommendation, he hesitated, saying that he was an obscure cardinal from the south of Poland that no one in the West had ever heard of. Nevertheless, he wrote us a letter of blessing. You can imagine our surprise when three years later he became Pope John Paul II, the leader of the Roman Catholic church.

In 1980, Pope John Paul II wrote and invited us to a special concert in the Vatican in Rome. On August 13, 1980 we sang to approximately 60,000 people. It was a great moment that I will never forget.

But one thing that impressed me was the fact that the personal secretary of the Pope, Monsignor Monduzzi, made sure that I was informed on the protocol necessary to meet a man of his station in life. He took me aside and instructed me in the ways that a Protestant addresses the Pope, what words were proper to use. I found this very interesting and it certainly set me at ease.

This process of protocol is necessary for meeting the leaders of countries worldwide. There is a protocol for meeting the Queen of England, for meeting the President of the United States. There also is a protocol for meeting the King of Kings, and that is to come into His presence with praise and singing.

Isaiah 60:18 speaks of the city of God, "thou shalt call thy walls Salvations, and thy gates Praise." God is surrounded in a city, by a wall that is called salvation. The way to get into that city is through the gate of praise. The book of Revelation tells us that there is no way to get into that city except by the gate, and every gate of access to heaven is called a gate of praise. There is no other way of access.

So many times Christians come before God, trying to gain His presence and an awareness of His presence, and they only bring their complaints and their problems and their requests. That is not the way of access.There is no access in coming that way. We don't get access to God by coming with petitions or supplications. We begin with praise. That is the way we get into His presence.

10

The Sacrifice Of Praise

The idea of sacrifice is everywhere in the Bible. The principle of sacrifice was first established in the Old Testament and began immediately after the original sin of Adam and Eve.

God required that Cain and Abel bring a sacrifice to Him. Abel offered the animal sacrifice that was pleasing to the Lord. Cain offered the Lord the first part of his harvest, the fruit of the ground, but this was unacceptable. As a result, Cain killed Abel out of jealousy.

The first murder in the Bible occurred because of religious division. It has become the pattern for the division between true faith and false faith throughout history. Those who would come to God with the fruit of their hands, have always been fighting those who come to God on the principle of faith. The spirit of Cain and the spirit of Abel are still alive in the Church today.

What is important to notice, however, is that *God required a sacrifice.* When God asked for a sacrifice He asked the people to bring the very best of their substance and to present it in a very specific manner to the Lord as an offering.

There were several sacrificial animals that were offered to God in the tabernacle of Moses. The high priest had to offer a bull for the cleansing of his own sin. A ruler of the people had to offer a ram. The people themselves could bring a lamb or goat. The poor people in Jesus' time often brought doves to the temple.

But the purpose for each sacrifice was the same. *God demanded the shedding of innocent blood for the covering of man's sin.* He instituted that principle when He shed the blood of innocent animals and took their skins to cover the nakedness of Adam and Eve in the garden. This is an awesome concept. God's holiness could not be violated. His holiness had to be propitiated. To do that, the blood of an innocent sacrifice had to be shed.

God's laws have not changed. When Jesus Christ died on the cross for our sin two thousand years ago, He propitiated the holiness of God. He satisified God's justice. The blood sacrifice performed at Calvary became the *final* sacrifice for man's sin.

Although the need for blood sacrifice was fulfilled at Calvary, the principle of sacrifice has not been abolished in the New Testament. The principle of sacrifice originated in the heart of God. God continues to require a sacrifice from His children. Hebrews 13:15 says, "let us offer the sacrifice of praise to God continually, that is, the fruit of our lips giving thanks to his name."

God knows that we must give in order to receive. He wants us to have abundance, but first He requires a sacrifice of some sort. This is what happens when we give unto the Lord. We make a sacrifice, we give until it hurts, and our sacrifice triggers the laws of God. God in return blesses us and we become the receivers of His abundance.

Abraham's trial of faith

Abraham and David clearly understood the principles of sacrifice. Abraham, the father of faith, walked with God for many years. When he was seventy-five years of age, God promised Abraham and Sarah that they would have a son. For twenty-four years they endeavored to believe God, but nothing happened.

Finally, they decided they would create their own solution. Abraham took to himself Hagar, the bond-maid, and Ishmael was born. Many of us would try to offer God an Ishmael when He demands an Isaac, a son of faith.

Finally, at ninety-nine years of age, God apppeared to Abraham and Sarah and told them they would have a son in one year. One year later Isaac was born. The name Isaac means laughter. It seems that Abraham and Sarah had laughed when God made the original pronouncement. But it was God who had the last laugh when Isaac was born.

Isaac was the joy of his father Abraham's heart. For years Abraham had looked out at the stars of the heavens, and gazed at the sands of the desert, and remembered the promise of God. God had said, "I will multiply thy seed as the stars of the heaven, and as the sand which is upon the sea shore." Now the promise had been fulfilled. Abraham's heart was full to overflowing. Never had there been a child as fine as Isaac. Never had a young man looked so handsome, stood so upright.

Then one day, as recorded in Genesis 22, God came to Abraham and said, "I want you to take Isaac, the son you love, and go to the land of Moriah. I want you to offer Isaac as a burnt offering upon one of the mountains." In absolute obedience, Abraham immediately saddled his animals, he took young men with him and his son and he went to the place that God had told him about. When they arrived at the mountain, Abraham said to the young men, "You stay here with the animals. I and the boy will go yonder and worship."

The heart of Abraham was heavy. He didn't know what was going to happen, yet he was willing to make the ultimate sacrifice. He was willing to give God the pride of his life, the joy of his heart, even though it seemed contrary to all the promises of God. Abraham was willing to obey God's voice.

As Isaac and his father went up the mountain, Isaac asked his father, "Where is the lamb?" Abraham turned and said, "My son, God will provide himself a lamb for a burnt offering." How profound those words were. God will provide himself a lamb. Jesus came as the eternal Lamb of God.

But notice the obedience of Abraham as he takes his son, builds an altar, lays the wood on the altar and then binds his son Isaac and lays him on the altar. Isaac was a young man. He easily could have overcome his father. But in obedience he lays on the altar. Abraham lifts the knife in the air above his son.

Suddenly, an angel of the Lord stops Abraham and tells him that God is pleased because Abraham has not withheld anything from the Lord. This is a classic example of true sacrifice. It is sacrifice of this kind that touches the heart of God. God was able to bless Abraham's seed and make of him a great people because Abraham understood God's principle of sacrifice. Abraham gave first and received after.

David and Ornan's offer

Another great example of sacrifice is seen in the life of David. In 2 Samuel 24 and 1 Chronicles 21, David, contrary to the command of God, had sinned in numbering the people of Israel. The wrath of God was kindled against him and the Lord sent a pestilence upon Israel. A death angel began to stretch his hand over Jerusalem to destroy it. The Bible says that David grieved and repented before God. God responded to David's repentance and commanded David to offer sacrifices in a special way and in a specific place.

The Lord said to build an altar on the threshing floor of Ornan the Jebusite. This was a challenge in disguise. Ornan was a farmer. He was in the midst of threshing wheat. If David were to build an altar in the middle of the threshing floor, that would shut down Ornan's threshing operation.

When Ornan realized the command of God to David, he immediately offered his threshing floor to David at no cost. He begged David to take the threshing floor and even offered his own oxen for burnt offerings and the threshing instruments for the wood of sacrifice.

David at this point was faced with a great temptation. Everything that God had demanded had been offered by Ornan. But David realized that the oxen, the threshing instruments, the threshing floor, all belonged to Ornan. *God had demanded a sacrifice of David, not of Ornan.* What a temptation this must have been for David. Here was an easy way to satisfy the demands of God without that sacrifice touching his own life.

How often this temptation comes to us. Our schedules get so busy. Our minds are occupied with the affairs of life. And when we come to the house of the Lord, we would prefer that the pastor, or the music director, or the choir make the sacrifice of worship for us.

David realized that the key of sacrifice involved himself. He had to make the sacrifice. *He realized it would be an insult to the character of God to offer sacrifices that had cost him nothing.* So David brought a sacrifice that was truly a sacrifice. David was a giver, not just a receiver. He understood the key, the underlying principle of all sacrifice. It must touch our flesh. *It is something we must do in spite of the way we feel.*

The high cost of sincere praise

There is a price to pay to enter into praise and worship. It is something that must touch our lives. There is a cost to this process. And yet each time we come to church we are faced with what I call "the offer of Ornan." There may be a liturgy. There may be beautiful choir music. The pastor may have an excellent message. It is so easy to settle back in the pew and enjoy the efforts of others. But God has commanded from us the sacrifice of praise.

That means it's going to cost us something. We are faced with a fundamental issue. Will we accept the "offer of Ornan," or will we enter into the sacrifice of praise?

God is not interested only in the praise that we give Him in times when things are going well. He is after that praise that comes in the midst of great trial, great difficulty, grief, sickness, demonic oppression, temptation, relational difficulties, and financial problems. He still requires praise. He still demands it. When we give it to Him in time of difficulty it means all the more to Him. *We are operating according to the principle of sacrifice, and God is pleased.*

The costliness of praise and sacrifice is illustrated in the tabernacle of Moses in the wilderness. Before the high priest came into the Holy of Holies to meet with God at the mercy seat, He came to the golden altar of incense immediately before the veil. It was necessary for the priest to offer incense on that altar before he walked through the veil. If he did not, he would be killed immediately.

The incense was very rare and costly. It was composed of four different ingredients gathered from different countries, and was blended in a unique fashion. No one was allowed to copy the ingredients in any other incense.

God demanded that sacrifice cost something. This is the principle that pleases Him, but it is the thing we try to avoid. We would far prefer to praise the Lord when it's easy for us. We would readily give Him our praises when things are going well. But God is more interested in our reactions as we walk through the trials of the fiery furnace. It is then that He requires the sacrifice. But it is precisely at this point that our greatest temptation comes upon us.

Conditioned by tradition

We have been trained to respond to God on the basis of feeling and not of faith. But praise is an act of the will. We *will* to praise God in spite of the way we feel. David said, "I *will* bless the Lord at all times: his praise shall [*will*] continually be in my mouth." But sometimes there is a great sacrifice involved in this act of the will. It is precisely at this point that our feelings and our will come into conflict.

In one of the many books written about the original Azuza Street revival in 1906, an author describes the beginnings of classical pentecostalism in the country. He describes the cultural traditions that have grown up in the pentecostal movement. These have not been articulated as doctrines, but have been passed from one generation to another. He states that pentecostals do not speak in tongues until they are "prompted." They do not enter into praise and worship until they are "prompted."

If this is true, it means that many pentecostals believe that speaking in tongues is more a function of emotion than of the will. This is wrong. We speak in tongues as an act of the will. It also is wrong in relationship to praise and worship. We praise God not only when we are prompted, but we praise the Lord at all times. Many of us have this cultural tradition to overcome. And the Devil knows how to make use of our cultural tradition.

Often, I used to sit in church services and watch the song leader or pastor on the platform encouraging everyone to stand up, clap, and raise their hands in public worship. If I didn't feel like it, I resented the efforts to get me to enter into the service. I stood in the congregation with my arms folded saying to myself, "I will not be hyped. I do not feel like praising God so I'm not going to do it."

I had been culturally conditioned by the concept that you didn't praise God until you were prompted by the Holy Spirit inside and felt like it. I would argue with myself and say, "Terry Law, you will not be a hypocrite. You don't feel like praising God, so don't praise Him. When you feel like it, then do it." So many times I missed out on the blessings of God because I was imprisoned by my feelings, rather than acting freely according to my own will.

Another problem in many charismatic churches is that people have been "into" praise and worship for so long that it has become merely a liturgical form. People raise their hands, say the right words, assume all the proper expressions of praise and worship, yet their minds are somewhere else. Their attention is not being directed toward the Lord, but is still involved in the affairs of life.

Disciplined to praise

Part of the sacrifice of praise is the directing of our thoughts toward the Lord. Our will literally grabs hold of our mind and focuses our attention upon the Word and upon the Lord. This involves sacrifice. This involves effort. But it must happen every time we come into the house of the Lord, or in our life on a day-by-day basis.

One verse in the Psalms has always intrigued me. In Psalm 103:1 David said, "Bless the Lord, O my soul: and all that is within me, bless his holy name." David is speaking to his soul. He is commanding his soul. He is saying, "Soul! Bless the Lord!" This is the essence of the sacrifice of praise. *It is absolutely necessary to teach every congregation the sacrifice of praise.*

When a church has learned the discipline of sacrifice, then they know when they gather together they have come to the house of God to praise. It is not necessary to inspire them with a hymn or with great choir music or with an exhortation. They have made a decision to come to the house of God and offer a sacrifice. When this begins to happen, the Spirit of the Lord comes upon the congregation and people are lifted into different dimensions of praise and worship. They prepare themselves for miracles.

Praise releases miracles

The sacrifice of praise is like turning a key in an automobile. It gets the engine started. The engine starts, the car begins to move. And in the same way the blessings of the Lord come down upon His people. Sacrifice brings miracles. When we are willing to make the sacrifice, we link ourselves directly to the miracle working power of God.

I know that if I stand in front of an audience, if they will follow me in the act of the sacrifice of praise, if they will openly and with a full heart begin to praise the Lord in spite of what they feel, we will see the miracle working power of God. There will be healing of the sick. People will be delivered from oppressing evil spirits. Relationships will be healed. Finances will be turned around. All of these things will happen. It is the principle of sacrifice that triggers the miracle working power of God.

When I lead a congregation into the sacrifice of praise like this, an incredible faith arises in my heart. I come to the point of praying the prayer of faith with great expectation. As I hear the sacrifice of praise from the people, I know beyond all shadow of a doubt that I'm going to see miracles. Never, in any miracle service that I have held, where people entered into a sincere sacrifice of praise, has there not been healing or manifestation of God's power.

An act of the will

Again, let me emphasize, it is the sacrifice that triggers the miracle. God has made us free-will moral agents with the ability to choose our own way. In giving us the power of choice, God had to risk that we would make the wrong choice. He gave us the opportunity of listening to God or the Devil. He gives us the permission to overcome the attacks of Satan with His Word. But the choice of doing that is ours.

The sacrifice of thanksgiving or the sacrifice of praise is the choice of every believer. It belongs to the will. It relates directly to the power of our free-will moral agency. That's why the business of the sacrifice of praise is fundamental to the life of a believer.

You cannot be successful as a Christian without recognizing the importance of your will in offering a sacrifice of thanksgiving and praise. Leviticus 22:29 says, "And when ye will offer a sacrifice of thanksgiving unto the Lord, offer it at your own will." Even under the law, God instituted the rule of thanksgiving. When Israel was commanded to bring an offering of thanksgiving, God specifically said, "You will bring it of your own free will."

They didn't have a choice in some of the things that God commanded them to do. But, when it came to thanksgiving, God told them that they must bring their free will into operation.

There is something about being willing to praise God that so pleases the heart of the Father. It is the sacrifice that He's after. It is a living sacrifice. It makes our lives holy, acceptable unto Him. In the Christian life we are sure of tests and trials as much as we are sure of death and taxes. They are going to come. The moment that insurmountable circumstances seem to surround us is actually an invitation from God to enter into the sacrifice of praise.

Don't allow the Devil to make you calloused and bitter. Don't allow him to turn you away from the Father. He will fill your mind with negative thoughts. He will do everything he can to erect strongholds inside of you. But it is precisely at this point that the sacrifice of thanksgiving and praise explodes in your spirit and leads you into the miracle working power of God.

When my wife Jan passed away, this is the primary principle that God taught me. My heart was aching. I was filled with grief. Bitterness and self-pity were beginning to enter my life. The Devil said, "God has been

very cruel to you. How could a loving God allow something like this." I was being bombarded with a series of
thoughts and strongholds, that were about to sink my
spiritual ship. I came to the point of one of the greatest
decisions of my life.

I got on my knees to pray and my words sounded
hollow. The Devil sat on my shoulder and whispered in
my ear and said, "Terry Law, you're a hypocrite. How
can you praise God when you hurt that bad inside." I
had to make a fundamental decision. The words of
David in Psalm 34:1 came to me at that moment, "I will
bless the Lord at all times: his praise shall continually be
in my mouth."

I made my choice. I said, "Devil I will bless the
Lord, and I command you to shut up. I command you
to leave my thoughts alone. I'm going to praise the
Lord. You can listen if you want but I'm still going to do
it." And then I entered into praise.

Nothing happened immediately. In fact it was two
hours later before I felt anything whatsoever. There
were two hours of barren praise. No emotion, no feeling, no tears, no sense of God or His presence. But I
said, "I will offer a sacrifice." And then the moment
came. There was an explosion in my spirit. The presence of God came into the room. And God initiated me
into the principles of the sacrifice of praise.

I know beyond all shadow of a doubt what God
will do in your heart if you will enter into this same
sacrifice. I know that you will see a miracle. I know that
there will be a sense of faith rise up inside of you greater
than you've ever had before. But you must make the
choice. Do it today. Let us offer the sacrifice of praise to
God continually.

11
Praise And Confession

The classic verse on the sacrifice of praise in the New Testament is Hebrews 13:15, "By him therefore let us offer the sacrifice of praise to God continually, that is, the fruit of our lips giving thanks to his name."

"The Amplified Version" of this verse states, "Through Him therefore let us constantly and at all times offer up to God a sacrifice of praise, which is the fruit of lips that thankfully acknowledge and confess and glorify His Name."[1]

In looking at this verse in other version's of the New Testament, I made an interesting discovery. The latter part of the verse in "The American Standard Version" says, "that is the fruit of lips which make confession to His name."[2] "The Berkley Version of the New Testament" translates it, "which is the fruit of lips that make confession in His name."[3]

A close examination of the original Greek indicates that the words "giving thanks" in the *King James* have been translated from the original Greek word *homologeo.* That word literally is translated in most other places in the New Testament as "to confess." The latter part of the verse should be correctly translated then, "that is the fruit of our lips confessing to His name."

This is a crucial distinction for us to make in this very important verse on praise and worship.

The writer to the Hebrews is telling us that in Christ, we are to offer a sacrifice of praise to God continually, that is, the fruit of our lips confessing to His Name. The sacrifice of praise therefore is equated in this verse as the fruit of our lips. It is something we do verbally. A sacrifice of praise must involve a vocal expression to God. That sacrifice of praise becomes then a confession to His Name.

What does that mean? The word *homologeo* in the *Expository Dictionary of New Testament Words* by W.E. Vine, is stated to mean, "to speak the same thing, to assent, agree with; to confess, declare, to confess by way of admitting oneself guilty; to confess or declare openly by way of speaking out freely, such confession being the effect of deep conviction of facts; *to confess by way of celebrating with praise.*"⁴

We have here a revelation of the connection between New Testament confession and the sacrifice of praise. Very few Christians realize the place that confession holds in the teaching of the New Testament. Jesus declared in Matthew 10:32, "Whosoever therefore shall confess me before men, him will I confess also before my Father which is in heaven." The concept of confession is also referred to in Rom. 10:9, 10; 1 Tim. 6:12; and Heb. 3:1.

Almost invariably, when the word confession is used, people think of confessing sin, iniquity, and transgression. That is the negative connotation of the word. But on the positive side, it means the confessing of our faith in God's Word. It is this positive kind of confession that the writer to the Hebrews is expressing. *Confession is saying the same thing with our mouth, that God says in His Word. It is literally making the words of our mouth agree with the written Word of God.*

In Psalm 116:10, the psalmist says, "I believed, therefore have I spoken." Paul uses this in his teaching in 2 Corinthians 4:13 and says, "We having the same spirit of faith, according as it is written, I believed and therefore have I spoken; we also believe, and therefore speak."

This is a description of the process of confession. If faith is going to move in our lives, it must have a means of expressing itself. The words of our lips give expression and life to the action of faith within us. Faith that does not speak is stillborn.

We speak what we believe

A close reading of Scripture reveals that there is a direct connection between our mouth and our heart. In Matthew 12:34 the Bible says, "for out of the abundance of the heart the mouth speaketh." Whatever is in our heart will find a way of expressing itself through our mouth. You can't separate the one from the other. The mouth is like a faucet that lets out what already is inside our hearts.

If our heart is filled with the Word of God, if we are standing in faith on what God's Word says, then that faith will be expressed out of our mouth. But, on the other hand, if we are filled with unbelief and fear, if we are bound by the strongholds of the Devil, then that will manifest itself by coming forth out of our mouth.

When Satan attacks us, he attacks us with thought-bombs. He endeavors to establish a stronghold in our lives through the thought process. He wants his evil thoughts to capture our heart. He wants those thoughts to go down inside of us. He wants them to be something that we believe in, meditate upon, and accept. The final goal of the Devil ultimately is to get hold of our mouth.

It is the mouth that is the center of spiritual warfare for the universe. Once the heart is captured, Satan knows that our mouth will speak out of the abundance of the heart. When he has control of the mouth, then he has control of the believer. He is able to throw his rockets of gossip, back-biting, divison, hatred, fear, lies, and so on. In doing this he has safely established his stronghold in our lives.

The more that our mouths confess the presence of the stronghold, the more the stronghold grips and controls us from the inside. Disease captures us exactly in this way.

Romans 10:8-10 deals with the subject of confession. Take note of the way mouth and heart appear in these verses (italics mine):

> **8 But what saith it? The word is nigh thee, even in thy *mouth*, and in thy *heart*: that is, the word of faith, which we preach;**
> **9 That if thou shalt confess with thy *mouth* the Lord Jesus, and shalt believe in thine *heart* that God hath raised him from the dead, thou shalt be saved.**
> **10 For with the *heart* man believeth unto righteousness; and with the *mouth* confession is made unto salvation.**

In verse 8, Paul mentions the mouth first, and the heart second. In verse 9, it is the mouth first and the heart second. But in verse 10, the order is reversed and the heart is mentioned first and the mouth second. This illustrates a very important scriptural principle. When we come to the Word of God and apply it against an attack of the Devil, the reality of Satan's stronghold is evident. We may be sick in our body, and endeavor to bring the Word of God against the sickness.

According to the pattern in these verses, it is necessary for us to begin by putting God's Word in our mouth as an act of our will, and bring it against the sickness. By confessing it, or saying the same thing with our mouth, as God says in his Word, we receive it into our heart. The more often we confess with our mouth, the more firmly it becomes established in our heart.

We believe what we speak

There comes a time then when the heart responds to what the mouth has been saying. The heart begins to believe the confession of the mouth. There is a moment of *rhema* revelation and the heart believes what the mouth is saying. Then the mouth naturally expresses what the heart is full of. This process is necessary for the reeducation of the heart. The confession of what God's Word says, is necessary to reeducate our mind.

In the Hebrew language the phrase "to learn by heart" actually is translated "to learn by mouth." This is how we learn best. I remember some of the poems that I had to learn in grade school. I repeated them over and over again with my mouth until I knew them in my heart.

This is the process of confession. If someone were to ask you the multiplicaton tables, you can repeat them because when you were a child you said them over and over again until they became a part of the understanding in your heart.

This is what happens with the Word of God. Every time we are attacked by the Devil, we come to God's Word and we begin to confess it. Obviously there is a struggle. The Word of God is saying something contrary to what we are experiencing. Our feelings will tell us that something is wrong, that God's Word cannot be true.

But the very process of confession demands that we resist our feelings and make the words of our mouth agree with God's Word. Sooner or later the struggle will be over and then it becomes a natural process for us to speak with our mouth exactly what God says in His Word.

The essence of confession is the same as that of the sacrifice of praise. Confession in this context becomes an act of the will rather than an act of the feelings. The sacrifice of praise literally is confessing to the Name of Jesus. Both the sacrifice of praise and confessing to the Name of Jesus proceed from an act of the will. Feelings cannot dictate to us. Feelings waver and will move us away from the truth of the Word.

There are some who obviously have taken the truth of confession in Scripture and abused it. It is easy for this kind of approach to degenerate into a mind over matter thing. Emile Coue told his followers to repeat daily, "Every day and in every way I'm getting better and better." Some have used the doctrine of confession as though God were a cosmic puppet that responds to us every time we pull His string.

The attitude of confession must be one of submission to the will of God and to the Scripture. We can only confess things in God's Word that are the expressed will of God for us. We must be led by the Spirit of God in our confession so that the confession can become a living *rhema.*

In Romans 10:10 Paul says, "For with the heart man believeth unto righteousness; and with the mouth confession is made unto salvation." The word "unto" indicates a motion or progress. In other words, we move progressively into the various elements of our salvation as we continue to make the right confession with our mouth. To understand what this means, we must understand the meaning of the term salvation.

In the New Testament the Greek verb *sozo* is usually translated "to save." But the meaning of this word goes far beyond the simple forgiveness of sins, that so many of us have attributed to it. A close examination of this term in the New Testament indicates that it means many things.

The total effect of salvation involves our deliverance from evil spirits. It involves the healing of our bodies and the raising from the dead. In fact, it sums up all of the benefits provided for us in the death of Jesus Christ on the cross.

Confession releases faith

Our confession is the doorway of our faith. It becomes the key that unlocks the wealth of God's promises on our behalf. This is an incredible truth that every believer must get hold of. We take hold of God's provision for us in every area of our life by entering into a confession.

The sacrifice of praise involves the confessing to His *Name. That is why I believe that the sacrifice of praise and worship will lead us into a total manifestion of the entire salvation provided for us on the cross by Jesus Christ.*

The sacrifice of praise essentially is an act of confession to the Word of God. The sacrifice of praise is saying the same thing with our lips as God says in His Word. The sacrifice of praise is taking the words of the Psalms, the words of the New Testament, and singing them, raising them as a triumphant anthem in the presence of God. By doing this, we move our feelings and the symptoms of our body into line with the declared Word of God, and we see a manifestion of the healing power of the Lord.

This is why in my meetings people are being healed consistently. As people enter the presence of God through the sacrifice of praise, their spirit is released to believe for the miracles of God. When an entire congregation does this; when everyone enters into the sacrifice, there is a massive confession flowing forth from an entire congregation. This massive confession moves against the power of strongholds that bind the minds and the bodies of God's children. A massive healing becomes the evidence of the confession of God's children.

Our praise, our triumphing in the power of God's Word ultimately means that the symptoms of disease will have to leave. We may waver, at first, and be caught in the tension between the symptoms and the unchanging truths of God's Word. But praise and worship will lead us into the victory.

The ministry of Jesus

In the book of Hebrews we have a main theme which accents the high priesthood of Jesus Christ. It really is a revelation of the ministry that Jeaus has at the right hand of the Father on our behalf. He ministers on our behalf to the Father. He offers prayers for us. He becomes a surety for the fulfillment of God's promises on our behalf. He is our personal representative.

A close reading of the book of Hebrews will reveal something else. *The high priesthood of Jesus Christ on our behalf, is directly linked to the confession of our mouths.* In other words, the confession that we make here on earth determines how much Jesus is able to minister on our behalf in heaven. He only goes as far as our confession permits Him.

In Hebrews 3:1 we are exhorted to consider Jesus Christ as the high priest of our confession. This links Christ's high priesthood directly to our confession. It is our confession that makes his priestly ministry effective on our behalf.

Each time we make the right confession we have the whole authority of Christ as our high priest behind us. He becomes surety of that which we confess. If we fail to make the right confession, if we confess doubt or unbelief, then Christ has no opportunity to minister as our high priest. Right confession invokes his priestly ministry on our behalf, but wrong confession shuts us off from it.

In Hebrews 4:14 the writer again links the high priesthood of Jesus directly to our confession. "Since then we have a great high priest who has passed through the heavens, Jesus the Son of God, let us hold fast our confession" (NASB). The emphasis here is in holding fast so that He will continue with His high priestly ministry.

Once we have brought the words of our mouth into agreement with God's written word, we must be careful not to change or go back to a position of unbelief. Many pressures may come against us, it may seem that all things are contrary to us, but by our faith and our confession we continue to hold onto those things which do not change.

In Hebrews 10:23 for the third time the writer stresses the connection between Christ's priesthood and our confession. Verse 21, "And having an high priest over the house of God ..." Verse 23 "Let us hold fast the profession [confession] of our faith without wavering."

In the three passages of Hebrews there is a mounting emphasis on the importance of maintaining a right confession. In Hebrews 3:1 we are told that Jesus is the high priest of our confession. In Hebrews 4:14 we are exhorted to hold fast to our confession. In Hebrews 10:23 we are exhorted to hold fast our confession without wavering.

The suggestion is that we are likely to be subjected to ever increasing pressures that would change or weaken our confession. Many of us can testify to the fact that this is true in our experience, therefore the warning is timely. No matter what pressures come, victory comes only through holding fast. In Hebrews 10:23 the promise is "for he is faithful that promised." Our confession links us to a high priest who cannot change.

As we look at the subject of confession and understand it, we can better understand Hebrews 13:15, "By him therefore let us offer the sacrifice of praise to God continually, that is, the fruit of our lips giving thanks [confessing] to his name." Praise is described in this verse as an act of confession to the name of the Lord. This could be defined as confessing the Name, confessing the Word and confessing the Blood. We are exhorted to offer this kind of sacrifice continually.

This indicates the tremendous force of praise in the life of the believer. *Your praise literally releases Jesus at the right hand of the Father to operate on your behalf.* Again, praise is the confession of our lips to the Name of Jesus. If we make the wrong confession, He has no opportunity to minister as our high priest.

That fact is awesome in its repercussions in the body of Christ. If we refuse to enter into praise and worship, then we refuse to allow Jesus to operate on our behalf at the right hand of the throne of the Father.

You see how tricky the Devil is? He tries to make your praise and worship dependent on how you feel. He would manipulate you with his "thought-bombs". He would do everything that he can, to tear you away from the act of praise.

He knows as soon as you enter into praise you will begin to confess the Word of God in your praise. You will use the Word as the weapon that God meant it to be. And as your praise and worship uses the weapon, it will begin to smash the strongholds of disease and bondage that the enemy puts upon you. So, therefore, the Devil tries to stop your praise, and in doing that he is stopping your confession. Therefore, Christ, the high priest of your confession, cannot work for you.

Hebrews 4:14 says, "Seeing then that we have a great high priest, that is passed into the heavens, Jesus the Son of God, let us hold fast our profession [confession]." We are exhorted to hold fast to our confession. That means we don't give up. That means we continue to insist that the written Word of God is true in our situation. We must hold fast to the Word in spite of everything.

Confession and praise

This must be applied equally to the subject of the sacrifice of praise. We must stand in the midst of our praise as surely as we must stand in the confession of our faith. The two are synonymous. They mean the same.

When we do this, immediately our high priest, Jesus Christ, goes to work at the right hand of the Father on our behalf. He offers our prayers to the Father. He acts as our personal representative in His presence. He presents our needs before the Lord, and then we watch the tremendous manifestation of His power in our midst. We begin to see the miracles. We see people set free, by the almighty power of God.

I am absolutely convinced that if you can see the truth of what I am saying here, *you will move into an area of faith unlike any you've known before.*

Through Christ, therefore, you offer the sacrifice of praise to God continually, every day, all the time. That is the fruit of your lips. Speak it out loud, and when you speak it you confess to the power of the Name of Jesus. This is the act of the sacrifice of praise. Your praise releases Jesus your high priest to minister on your behalf.

---

[1] *The Amplified Bible, New Testament.* Copyright © 1954, 1958 by The Lockman Foundation, La Habra, California.

[2] *The American Standard Version.* Copyright 1901 by Thomas Nelson & Sons and 1929 by International Council of Religious Education. Published by Thomas Nelson, Inc., Nashville, Tennessee.

[3] *The Modern Language Bible: The Berkeley Version In Modern English.* Copyright © 1945, 1959, 1969 by Zondervan Publishing House.

[4] W.E. Vine, *An Expository Dictionary of New Testament Words* (Old Tappan: Revell, 1966), vol. I, pp. 224.

12

The Mind's Battle With The Spirit

I am always amazed at the great difficulty most people have with praise and worship. There is something in the human personality that resists openly praising the Lord. Of course there are many cultural hang-ups that all of us face, especially involving verbal praise to the Lord. *But there seems to be an innate resistance toward the act of praise.*

Why is it so difficult to get a congregation to openly raise their voices, lift their hands, and praise the Lord unabashedly? What is there in the human mind, what tentativeness that makes us hold back and hesitate to enter into the act of praise?

The carnality of the mind

The Bible declares in Romans 8 that the carnal mind of man is actually in enmity against God. One of the great battles that everyone of us face, even after we become born-again and children of the Lord, is the battle with the carnal mind. Romans 8:5-7 says:

> 5 For they that are after the flesh do mind the things of the flesh; but they that are after the Spirit the things of the Spirit.
> 6 For to be carnally minded is death; but to be spiritually minded is life and peace.

> 7 Because the carnal mind is enmity against God: for
> it is not subject to the law of God, neither indeed can
> be.

Paul then goes on throuhout Romans 8 to define the battle between flesh and Spirit. It is interesting to note in verses 5 through 7 that the flesh is in enmity against the Spirit, but in verse 6 Paul ties the mind directly to the flesh. It's important to see the connection between mind and flesh here. Verse 12 and 13 state:

> 12 Therefore, brethren, we are debtors, not to the
> flesh, to live after the flesh.
> 13 For if ye live after the flesh, ye shall die: but if ye
> through the Spirit do mortify the deeds of the body,
> ye shall live.

The carnal mind and the body are tied into the acts of the flesh. *Paul is outlining a battle that takes place between the mind and the Spirit.*

The first three chapters of the Bible tell the story of God creating man. The Bible states in Genesis 2:7, "And the Lord God formed man of the dust of the ground, and breathed into his nostrils the breath of life; and man became a living soul." You have in this verse all three aspects of man. You have his body formed of the dust of the ground, his spirit inbreathed by the breath of God, and the fact that when body and spirit came together man became a living soul.

God commands Adam in Genesis 2:16, 17, "Of every tree of the garden thou mayest freely eat: But of the tree of the knowledge of good and evil, thou shalt not eat of it: for in the day that thou eatest thereof thou shalt surely die."

One of the first gifts God gave to man was the ability to communicate, to talk with God. God placed man in a home which He called Eden. God gave Adam the ability to dress, tend, and keep the garden. In that garden there was no discord, no sickness, no sin, no disharmony. God made man a home where they could fellowship together. But another voice came into the garden. The Devil arrived and sowed a discordant note in Eden; his voice was out of tune.

God had showed His trust in man by placing him in the garden and giving him all legal rights to everything in the garden. To all the fruit of the trees except one. Now, in order for man to be a man, he had to be a person of choice. He had to be able to say yes or no, to respond or to react to God.

Seeing the possibility of choice in man the serpent seized upon it. He struck at man and planted a seed of doubt. He made man doubt the goodness of God. The serpent said to Eve, "Yea, hath God said, Ye shall not eat of every tree of the garden?" Then the Devil contradicted the Word of God and said "Ye shalt not surely die."

The Devil told a half-truth, he was referring to physical death while God was talking about the death of the human spirit. When God said "Ye shall surely die" He was speaking of the spiritual-moral image of Himself in man.

In other words, when man ate of the tree of the garden, his spirit would die. It would not cease to exist, *but the Spirit of God that gave life to man would depart and he would be spiritually dead.* When Adam and Eve made their choice and ate of the tree of the knowledge of good and evil, man fell. But notice in this battle for the spirit of man, how Satan appealed to man's mind. He reasoned with the mind of Eve. He appealed to her intelligence. *Satan put the mind of man in opposition to his spirit.*

The spirit of Adam and Eve knew fellowship with God. The Devil knew that if he could create an internal disharmony he would get the soul of man. In the original sin we see a rebellion in the wholeness of man.

Because of the original sin, the battle between mind and spirit still rages inside of man. Our minds want to control us. So the flesh, or the mind, is in constant battle with the spirit. The flesh would have us go contrary to the leading of the Spirit.

The spirit of man naturally wants to fellowship with God. The spirit of man knows that praise is the coin of the realm of the Spirit. God is a Spirit so it is natural for the spirit of man to worship through the Spirit of God.

Worship is the function of the human spirit in relation to God the Father. But the mind would do battle with us at this point. The carnal mind is at enmity against God. That's why Paul in Romans 12:2a says, "Be not conformed to this world: but be ye transformed by the renewing of your mind."

When a man is saved, his mind is not necessarily renewed instantaneously. He will have many of the same thought patterns that he had before salvation. He will find the temptations that came to him before will still come. The mind has not yet been renewed. The mind must be renewed by the Word of God. The mind must be renewed by the Spirit of God. The mind must be renewed by praise and worship.

Praise can lead us across the bridge from the mind into the spirit. Praise is putting down the mind. Praise is putting down the feelings. Praise is an act of the will. Praise says, "I will bless the Lord at all times, his praise shall continually be in my mouth." Praise is an invitation to the human spirit to flow in worship to God.

That is why when we come into a church service and we encourage the people to worship the Lord, there is this initial resistance. It takes an extra push to get the "wagon rolling." Our minds have been deep in our business, in the affairs of family, concerned with the circumstances of life. When we come to the house of the Lord, the mind must be taken off the throne and we must give the throne to the spirit. We have come to the house of the Lord to worship God, so the spirit must have preeminence.

The mind fights us at this point. It is only as we enter into praise by an act of our will, literally launch ourselves into the business of praise, that the mind is put in its place and the spirit is given the preeminence it must have.

Bridging the communication gap

One of the first gifts God gave to man was the ability to communicate freely, to talk with God. We have a mouth, we have vocal organs, we have a tongue, we have the ability to praise because praise and worship involves talking to God. Man is made to communicate. In the Garden of Eden, God and man walked and talked together. This is worship. This is the beginning of the praise and worship process. Man is made to praise and worship.

It is absolutely fundamental that we understand that before any communication between God and man transpires, praise and worship must exist and to do this talking must take place.

Jesus came as the second Adam to reestablish communication between God and man. Jesus said at the end of his life, "I must go away, but I'm going to send you the Holy Spirit. It's better for you that I send you the Holy Spirit because he is with you now, but he shall

be in you" (John 16:7, John 14:17b, author's para-
phrase). Jesus knew that the Holy Spirit would again
create this ability for communication between God and
man. The Holy Spirit would build the bridge between
the mind and the spirit and make man able to fellowship with the Father.

In the Upper Room on the day of Pentecost the
Holy Spirit was outpoured. All were filled with the
Holy Spirit and spoke with other tongues as the Spirit
gave them utterance.

The Holy Spirit came to restore togetherness with
God, to make it possible for man to communicate freely
with God. That is the purpose for the prayer language
of the spirit. We do not speak in tongues for the sake of
emotion to release something that is pent-up within us.
We do not speak in tongues so that we have a doctrinal
distinctiveness that separates us from other believers.
Praying in tongues is communication. It is a bridge between the mind and the spirit that relates us directly to
God.

It is very clear in the life of the apostle Paul that he
was filled with the Spirit. He said, "I speak with
tongues more than you all." He emphasized the importance of the bridge between man and God, the bridge
between man's mind and his spirit. Paul says in 1 Corinthians 14:15, "What is it then? I will pray with the
spirit, and I will pray with the understanding also."

It's important to know that Paul prayed with his
spirit. That is, he prayed in tongues, the prayer language of the spirit. Down deep, in the deepest levels of
his existence, where he was lonely, he prayed with his
spirit. The Holy Spirit gave Paul's spirit the power to
pray. Paul was using his tongue to speak the words of
God like one would use a faucet to turn on water. His

spirit was speaking to God in ways that his mind could not express.

Then notice Paul says, "I will pray with the understanding also." After he had prayed with the prayer language of the spirit, he paused and waited for God to give him the interpretation, to know what his spirit had prayed. God's response came back through Paul's mind or understanding. It gave him release and his spirit was edified and lifted up.

Spirit speaking with spirit

In 1 Corinthians 14:2, Paul states, "For he that speaketh in an unknown tongue speaketh not unto men, but unto God: for no man understandeth him; howbeit in the spirit he speaketh mysteries." In 1 Cor. 2:11, he states, "For what man knoweth the things of a man, save the spirit of man which is in him? even so the things of God knoweth no man, but the Spirit of God." The spirit of man needs to know the things of the Spirit of God, so a bridge has to be built between God and man.

The divine bridge that God has provided for the believer is the bridge of the prayer language, speaking in other tongues. When we speak in an unknown tongue we don't speak to man, we are speaking to God. The prayer language is the communication vehicle ordained by God for the believer. It takes man back to the Garden of Eden. Man comes into the original act of fellowship with God that Adam and Eve had with the Lord. This is true praise and worship.

The Day of Pentecost is described in Acts 2. Those gathered in the upper room began speaking in tongues. All who witnessed this were amazed and marvelled saying, "Behold, are not all these that speak Galileans? And how hear we every man in our tongue wherein we were born?"

Then it lists the various races of people that were there, and the explanation is given, "We do hear them speak in our tongues [or, dialect] the wonderful works of God [or, the things that God has done]." *It is obvious that the original act of praying in the spirit was an act of praise and worship.*

In looking at the spiritual launching rockets of the believer, each one of them is an individual act having to do with the mouth. Prayer proceeds out of the mouth. Preaching proceeds out of the mouth. Testimony proceeds out of the mouth. Praise and worship proceed out of the mouth.

The mouth is the center of spiritual warfare for the entire universe. Think of the spiritual battling we are doing when we pray in the spirit. Think of the praise and worship that is going forth to the Father. Think of the strongholds that are being attacked and torn down as we spend time flowing in our prayer language. Most believers introduced into the baptism of the Holy Spirit never give God the quality time praying in tongues they ought to.

At this point, let's take a look at the way Paul understood the difficulty between mind and spirit. In 1 Corinthians 2:9, Paul says these words, "Eye has not seen, nor ear heard, neither have entered into the heart of man, the things which God hath prepared for them that love him."

An alternate word for heart, here, would be mind. The phrase, "The things that God hath prepared for them that love him," is the key phrase for the next several verses. Paul refers to those things on several different occasions. He declares in verse 9 that our eyes haven't seen, and our ears haven't heard, neither has it entered into our mind, what God has prepared for us.

What are the things that God has prepared for them that love Him? I used to believe that Paul was referring here to life after death. However, the context indicates that he is referring to blessings available to the believer right now.

God has prepared many things for them that love Him. He has prepared the new birth. He has prepared freedom from condemnation. We have been made new creatures in Christ Jesus. He has provided healing for the believer according to 2 Peter 2:24, and Matthew 8:17. Prosperity is the believer's blessing according to 2 Corinthians 9:8. Justification, reconciliation, redemption, all these are things that God has prepared for them that love Him.

But notice Paul's statement that our senses don't understand these things. Our eyes, ears and mind do not understand the things of God. He goes on in verse 10, "But God hath [past tense] revealed them unto us by his Spirit." It is the Spirit of God that has revealed unto the spirit of man the things that God has prepared for them that love Him.

Paul is putting the mind and spirit of man in contra-distinction. Our minds don't understand those things, our spirit does. Our minds may understand them after our spirit reveals them to the mind, but it is truly the spirit that understands.

Verse 11 states, "For what man knoweth the things of a man, save the spirit of man which is in him?" Paul says here, it is our human spirit that really understands the truth about us. If you are suffering a problem in your marriage, your mind will try to figure it out, but the answer to that problem is in the human spirit. "Even so the things of God knoweth no man, but the

Spirit of God." That phrase is self explanatory.

Verse 12 declares, "Now we have received, not the spirit of the world, but the Spirit which is of God; that we might know the things that are freely given to us of God." Why have we received the Spirit which is of God? Solely that we might know those things that are freely given to us of God. Paul is referring immediately back again to the statement made in verse 9. "Our eyes can't see, nor our ears hear, nor our minds understand, the things that God has prepared for them that love Him."

We have received the Spirit of God so that we might know those things. God wants us to know the power of His spiritual truth. He wants us to know justification, healing, redemption, etc. That is why we have the Spirit of God within us. *It is the craving of the Holy Spirit of God within you to show you the great things that God has freely given to you.*

You don't understand healing in your mind. You may understand the doctrine that way, but healing is apprehended in your spirit. *It is the spirit that grabs hold of healing and translates it into physical action in your body.*

Verse 13 says, "Which things also we speak." What things is Paul referring to here? The things that are freely given to us by God. Paul says, "I can preach about those things, but I don't do it in the words which man's wisdom teaches but which the Holy Ghost teaches."

Verse 14 continues, "But the natural man receiveth not the things of the Spirit of God." This means the soulish man, the man who is focused on his mind. This man cannot receive the things of the Spirit of God. He does not accept them. They are foolishness unto him.

The only way that he can know them is through spiritual discernment, which he does not have.

The essence of what Paul says in this portion is that we have received the Spirit of Almighty God, so that we might know the things that God has freely given to those that love Him. It is the Spirit that understands. Therefore, we must come to the Spirit so that we might understand.

Praise uses words. Praise uses the mouth. It involves the human tongue. When, by an act of our will, we decide to praise the Lord, we bring our tongue into line with the Word of God. We bring our tongue into line with the explosive power of God.

We are preparing ourselves to use our prayer language. We are telling our mind to be quiet. We are giving preeminence to the spirit. We are reversing the course of our human nature. We are saying to our spirit, "I want you to flow in worship to God. I want that bridge of communication established between me and God, my Father. I am going to praise the Lord. I will lift my voice. I will use my tongue. I will open my mouth."

Praise from the mouth of man literally shuts up the Devil, brings healing, deliverance, prosperity, freedom from the problems that plague the family, and deliverance from the oppression of evil spirits. Praise is the key.

13

Praise And Angels

It is impossible to read the Bible without being impressed by the fact that angels have a great part in the business of praise. Revelation 5:11, 12 states, "And I beheld, and I heard the voice of many angels round about the throne and the beasts and the elders: and the number of them was ten thousand, times ten thousand and thousands of thousands; Saying with a loud voice, Worthy is the Lamb that was slain to receive power, and riches, and wisdom, and strength, and honour, and glory, and blessing."

Angels always have been involved in praise unto the Lord. Angels sang God's glory announcing Jesus' birth in Bethlehem. At the beginning of creation it says in Job 38:7, "The morning stars sang together and all the sons of God shouted for joy." The phrase "the sons of God" refers to angels. Angels have been very much involved with the business of praise.

In Isaiah's vision, he sees the seraphim and the cherubim praising God in the temple. If angels are so involved in praise and worship to God, what relationship does the praise of the body of Christ have to that of angels?

The Bible indicates in Hebrews 12:22, 23, "But ye

are come unto mount Sion, and unto the city of the living God, the heavenly Jerusalem, and to an innumerable company of angels, To the general assembly and church of the firstborn, which are written in heaven, and to God the Judge of all." It is obvious that before God in heaven, the angel's praise intermingles with the praise of the Church.

The warfare of angels

In 2 Kings 6, the king of Syria was upset because his private counsels were known, and he was informed that Elisha, the prophet in Israel, was able to read the thoughts of his mind. The king invaded Dothan where Elisha was staying.

When Elisha's servant got up one morning, he saw the invading army of Ben-Hadad, the king, that had come at night, and he was very upset. He said, "Alas, my master! how shall we do?" But Elisha said to the servant, "Fear not: for they that be with us are more than they that be with them." Elisha prayed and said, "Lord, I pray thee, open his eyes, that he may see." And the Lord opened the eyes of the young man and he saw the mountain was full of horses and chariots of fire.

The armies of the Lord constantly are doing battle on behalf of God's children. Psalms 34:7, says, "The angel of the Lord encampeth round about them that fear him, and delivereth them."

Angels often are involved in carrying out the judgement destruction orders of the Lord. When Lot was called by God to come out of Sodom, the Lord sent angels to deliver Lot and his wife and children. In Genesis 19, we have the story of the angels' destruction of the city of Sodom. They literally destroyed the city of Sodom in response to the command of God. Angels smote Herod because of his sin against God and the

Bible says he was eaten of worms and died.

In Psalms 35, when David speaks of His enemies, he says, "let the angel of the Lord chase them, let the angel of the Lord persecute them." So it is obvious that the angels are involved in carrying out the judgement commands of God. They are involved in spiritual warfare, but they also are involved in praise.

Joint warfare

Revelation 12:7-11 describes a war in heaven that takes place in the future. It involves God's angels working with believers in the casting down and defeat of Satan and his angels:

> 7 And there was war in heaven: Michael and his angels fought against the dragon; and the dragon fought and his angels,
> 8 And prevailed not; neither was their place found any more in heaven.
> 9 And the great dragon was cast out, that old serpent, called the Devil, and Satan, which deceiveth the whole world: he was cast out into the earth, and his angels were cast out with him.
> 10 And I heard a loud voice saying in heaven, Now is come salvation, and strength, and the kingdom of our God, and the power of his Christ: for the accuser of our brethren is cast down, which accused them before our God day and night.
> 11 And they overcame him by the blood of the Lamb, and by the word of their testimony; and they loved not their lives unto death."

It is clear from the entire context that believers *and* God's angels were involved together in the battle against Satan and his forces. It was a joint effort. *Notice in verse seven, it was Michael and his angels that cast Satan down. But, in verse eleven, it was believers that overcame by the Blood and the word of their testimony.* What does this mean?

The believers made use of their weapons and of their spiritual launching rockets. The weapon used in this particular instance was the Blood of Jesus, or the Blood of the Lamb. They overcame the Devil by the Blood of the Lamb. This verse is a tremendous representation of the weapon and spiritual launching rocket of the believer. *They overcame the Devil by the Blood of the Lamb and by the word of their witness or testimony.*

Testimony or witness is the vital launching rocket used by the believers in overcoming the Devil. The Blood is the weapon, but testimony is what launched the weapon. *It appears that the spiritual activity of the believers on the earth is coordinated with the activity of the angels of God in heaven.*

I think it is logical to assume that Michael and his angels could have fought against the dragon and his angels anytime they wanted. If God had told Michael to cast them out of heaven he would have cast them out. However, it is interesting to notice that believers cooperated with angels in the actual casting down of the Devil.

It appears that the angels were waiting for believers to get active in spiritual warfare before they actually carried out the spiritual equivalent of what the believers had been praying for.

Am I saying that believers control angels? Absolutely not. I believe that angels can only be obedient to the voice of God the Father. He is the One who commands them. I do believe, however, that when believers start moving in the plan of God and principles of Scripture in terms of spiritual warfare, then angels are freed by God to do what they have always wanted to do. The angels will not begin to move on our behalf against the powers of darkness until the Church begins to recognize its authority and takes the position God originally meant it to take.

Let us take a look at another story from the Old Testament in Daniel the tenth chapter. This chapter offers an unusual glimpse of spiritual warfare. Daniel had been a captive in the land of Babylon for 70 years. In the 9th chapter of Daniel, the Bible says that Daniel was reading the book of Jeremiah. As he read the book of the prophet he realized that Jeremiah had prophesied that Israel would be held 70 years in captivity in Babylon.

Daniel remembered Jeremiah from his boyhood days. Jeremiah had been that eccentric prophet who walked through the streets of Jerusalem prophesying destruction on the city, prophesying that one day Nebuchadnezzar and Babylon would move against the city and destroy it.

As Daniel read through the book he noticed that Israel would be held captive for 70 years. A quick look at the calendar revealed that the 70 years had come to an end. Daniel immediately began a time of fasting and prayer. As Daniel sought the Lord and asked God to restore Israel back to the city of Jerusalem, an angel of the Lord appeared to Daniel. It was Gabriel the great messenger angel of God who came to speak with him and bring him a message from the Lord.

In verse 12 of chapter 10, the angel said, "Fear not, Daniel: for from the first day that thou didst set thine heart to understand, and to chasten thyself before thy God, thy words were heard, and I am come for thy words." The angel makes an interesting comment here. The indication is that the angel was sent by God immediately when Daniel began to pray and that the angel was sent in relationship to the words of Daniel. Now what words were these?

Notice in the previous chapter Daniel had been reading from the book of Jeremiah. As he read the words of Jeremiah's prophecy he began to pray those words to the Lord. He reminded God of His promise in the Word. Daniel began to pray the inspired Word of God and as he prayed the Word of God, those words were heard by the Father immediately. Then Gabriel was dispatched to Daniel with a message from the Lord.

Notice the angel was sent the first day. As soon as the first prayer was prayed he was dispatched. Daniel's prayer, based on the prophecy of Jeremiah had instantaneous response. However, Gabriel was intercepted by an evil power called the prince of the kingdom of Persia. It is interesting that this prince had the ability to withstand Gabriel the archangel of God for one and twenty days. That raises a question in the mind.

How could the prince of Persia withstand Gabriel for one and twenty days? He must have been a powerful being. However, when Michael arrived, Gabriel was freed to get to Daniel with the message.

A close examination of the role of Michael and Gabriel as angels indicates that Gabriel is a messenger angel. It was Gabriel who was sent to Mary and Joseph, and Zachariah announcing the birth of Jesus and John the Baptist. Michael however is not a messenger angel. He is a warrior angel and later on in this chapter he is named as the prince responsible for the destiny of Israel.

When it comes to military action, Michael is used, not Gabriel. As soon as Michael arrived, Gabriel was freed to come to Daniel. If Gabriel started to Daniel on the first day but didn't arrive until the twenty-first day because of spiritual warfare in the heavenlies, what would have happened if Daniel had not kept on praying?

Is it possible that when we begin to pray according to the Word; that when we begin to exercise spiritual warfare according to divine principles, that angels begin to respond to our prayers? Is it possible that when we give up and stop before the angel has arrived, they are not able to carry out the commands of almighty God because we have not exercised our authority as the church of Jesus Christ? I personally believe that if Daniel had quit praying, the angel would have turned around and gone back.

Notice the power of the prince of Persia to withstand Gabriel. This is a true example of spiritual warfare. It is interesting that this great evil power is called the prince of the kingdom of Perisa.

Paul says in Ephesians 6:12, "For we wrestle not against flesh and blood, but against principalities ..." That word is arché in the Greek. It refers to the first among rulers and obviously is a direct reference to the prince that Daniel faced in his prayer. Paul says we wrestle with princes.

This is where the real battle in spiritual warfare takes place. The point to understand here is this. This scripture says that Daniel's words were heard. Daniel exercised the principles of spiritual warfare correctly. The weapon that Daniel used was the Word of God. He prayed the prophecy of Jeremiah, he brought it before the Lord.

Launching prayer

The launching rocket used by Daniel was prayer. His twenty-one days of fasting only added to the keenness and to the power of prayer. Prayer, as a launching rocket, is greatly enhanced and empowered by fasting. Daniel's weapon was the Word of Jeremiah. The launching rocket was prayer. What happened in the area of the heavenlies is the surprising thing. Angels moved in response to the spiritual warfare of God's man on the earth.

Obviously the man didn't command the angels. The angels were commanded by God. *When God's children move on the principles of the authority that God has granted to them, angels begin to cooperate with them in spiritual warfare.*

In 2 Chronicles 20 we have the story of the invasion of Israel by three armies. Jehoshaphat is the king of Israel, and when he is informed of the invasion, the Bible says that Jehoshaphat feared. He began seeking the Lord and proclaimed a fast throughout all of Judah. Jehoshaphat prayed a great prayer before the people. At the end of his prayer the spirit of prophecy came upon Jahaziel, a Levite. His prophetic word outlined the battle plan that God had for the next day.

God certainly gave a very unusual plan of attack. The plan was for the Levites to lead the army into battle. The Levites were the professional musicians of the temple. It was the Levites that God wanted marching in front of the armies of Israel. When you understand the principles of spiritual warfare, it is easy to understand the unusual results of this story.

The Levites advanced before the armies of Israel, praising and worshipping the Lord with songs. Notice their use of spiritual warfare here by direct command of God. When God needs to fight a battle, this is the way God fights. He's not interested in the might of the oncoming army. He's not interested in how much armor they have or how much firepower. He deals in the area of spiritual warfare. He binds the strongholds. He looses His authority through His people so that *the battle is won in heavenly places before there is a physical manifestation of it here on the earth.*

The launching rocket that was used by the children of Israel was praise and worship. The weapon that was used was the Name. They praised the Name of the Lord. They were overwhelmed with the holiness and power of the Name of the Lord. They uplifted that in their praise. As soon as they began to sing and to praise, the Lord set ambushments against the three armies of the enemy.

The Lord's ambushments

How does God set ambushments? In order to understand ambushments, we must go to other stories of the Bible. Remember when Balaam disobeyed the Lord and God was angry with him? He sent an angel to carry out His vengeance. Balaam's donkey saw the angel but Balaam did not. When the Lord finally opened the eyes of Balaam, he saw the angel and fell on his face. God sets ambushments with angels.

Remember the story of Elisha at Dothan when the eyes of his servant were opened and he saw that they who were with Elisha were more than they who were with the enemy? There were more angels of God with Elisha and his servant than there were evil angels with the invading hosts of the Assyrians under Ben-Hadad the king. The mountain was full of horses and chariots of fire. Again, in Psalm 35, David speaks of his enemies. He says, "Let the angel of the Lord chase them."

When God sets ambushments, He does it with angels. *Notice their ambushments coincided exactly with the time that the children of Israel began to sing and to praise. It was praise that loosed the angels.* The angels of God had the power to destroy the strongholds that were influencing the invading enemy. But they did not overcome them until God's children had exercised the principles of spiritual warfare in the correct manner. Then, the angels confounded the enemy in a unique manner and they destroyed themselves.

It is very possible that the angels whispered in the ears of the invading armies and sowed the seeds of doubt and suspicion in their minds so that they self-destructed.

It is sensible to believe that if the Devil's angels can sow thoughts of disease, bondage, and fear in our minds, the angels of God can sow seeds of confusion in the minds of the Devil's children. However, the point to note is that angels responded to God's children when they exercised the correct principles of spiritual warfare.

Praise changes history

In Acts 12, Herod killed James, the brother of John, with a sword. Then he put Peter in prison, "but prayer was made without ceasing of the church unto God for Peter." The Church immediately began to intercede for Peter. What happened? The angel of the Lord came to Peter in the prison, delivered him, and set him free from the jail. This indicates the connection between the prayer of God's children and the activity of angels.

This revelation presents great possibilities in the story of the imprisonment of Paul and Silas described in Acts 16. Paul and Silas exercised the principles of spiritual warfare and literally praised the Lord in a loud voice so that the prisoners could hear them.

Suddenly there was an earthquake. Is it not possible that their praise to the Lord released the angels of

God and gave them the freedom to do what they wanted to do in terms of shaking the foundations of the prison? Imagine the angels, perhaps four of God's best, standing around that prison, one at each corner, shaking the daylights out of the prison! It is a possibility, is it not?

I don't think the Church today has even the faintest idea of the great potential that praise has in spiritual warfare. The authority is delegated to the Church. We must move with that authority in order for the Church to establish the kingdom of God here on the earth. If God will not move until we move, then our job is to celebrate the triumph of Christ in spoiling principalities and powers.

When we get in the chariot, when we lift our voices, when we enter into praise and worship, celebrating the fact that the power of principalities and powers has been broken; then the angels of God are loosed on our behalf to perform exploits for the Church. What they want to do for us is overwhelming. One day they will cast Satan out of the second heaven in response to the exercise of spiritual warfare by believers.

One man, Daniel, was able to influence the history of an entire nation because he exercised spiritual warfare correctly. What great promise this offers for everyone of us through praise and worship. If we enter mightily, throw ourselves whole-heartedly into praise and worship, is it not possible that an angel will work with us in standing against the strongholds that try to bind us.

Our standing in praise and worship will help bring the angel on the scene with a manifestation of the mighty, miracle working power of almighty God? Daniel's prayer did it. So can ours. However, we must begin to catch the revelation of the authority that Christ has delegated to the Church.

The believer's authority

The word "power" in the New Testament comes from several Greek root words, *dunamis, exousia,* and others. When Jesus said, "all power is given unto me in heaven and in earth," the word used is *exousia.* It means authority.

I once read a story of a group of young Mexican Boy Scouts who were trying to cross the Avenue Reforma, a great boulevard in the heart of Mexico City. It was during the time of rush hour traffic. Mexico City's rush hour traffic is close to the most hectic anywhere in the world.

The boys made it half-way across the broad street and took refuge on the *esplanade* in the street's center. On the *esplanade* there was a special tall chair, or pedestal, where the traffic officer stood to direct traffic. The boys watched as the traffic officer would raise his right hand and all the powerful speeding automobiles would screech to a halt. In Mexico City that pedestal is a place of authority and all the motorists knew it.

About this time, a slight accident occurred nearby and the officer left his place to investigate. While he was arguing with the motorist, one of the Boy Scouts stepped up on the pedestal and raised his right hand. Instantly, cars began to grind to a halt.

The motorists recognized that the boy was standing in the place of authority. The boy could not physically stop those powerful automobiles. But the motorists were compelled to stop, even when a small boy stood in the place of authority, because the power of the government of Mexico was represented by the place upon which he stood.

The greatest power in the universe stands behind the believer. When Jesus said, "all authority has been given unto me in heaven and in earth," and then in the next verse said, "go ye therefore," He was talking to the disciples. He was addressing His words to the Church. He was saying, "I have the authority and I delegate that authority to you. Go ye therefore and preach the Gospel." *God has delegated to the Church a great authority.* God Himself is the force behind the authority. *The believer who is thoroughly conscious of the divine power behind him can face the enemy without fear or hesitation.*

Behind the authority possessed by the believer is a power greater than our enemy's. God has delegated authority to the Church. He is waiting for the Church to exercise the authority delegated to her. This is not something that God is *going* to do. He *already* has done it. Jesus is at the right hand of the Father, at the place of authority, and we are seated with Him. Now we are to carry out the activity of the Head of the Church.

In Ephesians, Christ is defined as the head, and the Church as the body. Your head and your body are one. Christ has delegated authority on the earth to the Church. All the authority that can be exercised upon the earth has to be exercised through the Church.

Problems exist because we permit them to, because we have not entered into the principles of spiritual warfare. The problems exist not because God winks at them, but because He has given us the authority and we have not exercised the authority. We are responsible for carrying out His work on the earth as the Church.

People often ask why God lets the Devil do bad things on the earth. There is no place in the epistles where any writer tells the believer to pray to God the

Father about the Devil. People who ask God to rebuke the Devil are wasting their time. The most insignificant member of the body of Christ has just as much power over the Devil as anyone else. Unless believers do something about the Devil, nothing will be done.

Various Scriptures indicate the authority given to us in spiritual warfare. In Mark 16, we are commanded to go into the world and preach the gospel, then signs shall follow, "In My name shall they cast out devils; they shall speak with new tongues; they shall lay hands on the sick," and so forth. These verses indicate that the authority over the Devil lies with the Church. James 4:7 says, "Resist the devil, and he will flee from you." *You* is the understood subject of the sentence. *You* are supposed to resist the Devil. The text doesn't say he'll flee from Jesus. It says he will flee from *you.* The authority is yours.

Feeling has nothing to do with it. It's like the little boy in Mexico. When he held up his hand the traffic stopped. No matter how weak we are, when we understand our authority and raise our hand the Devil stops.

Another Scripture is 1 Peter 5:8, 9a, "Be sober, be vigilant; because your adversary the devil, as a roaring lion, walketh about, seeking whom he may devour: Whom resist steadfast in the faith ..." *We must resist the Devil.* Ephesians 4:27 says, "neither give place to the devil."

Don't give the Devil any place in your life. If you give place to the Devil in your life, there is nothing Jesus can do because *you* have the authority and *you* have given the Devil permission. *By the very principles of delegation God does not move or operate without the Church.*

A Church victorious

Jesus said in Luke 10:19, "Behold, I give unto you power [or authority] to tread on serpents and scorpions, and over all the power of the enemy: and nothing shall by any means hurt you." The Devil's been walking on us much too long. We have been given authority to tread on him. We are to reign as kings in life.

Believers are going to rise up and stand upon the principles of spiritual warfare. They are going to exercise their authority as the members of the body of Christ. The Church will do the job. God is not building a defeated Church. We're going to win the battle. The Church will be victorious against the Devil. The gates of hell shall not prevail against the Church of Jesus Christ.

I used to think that meant that the gates of hell were crashing against the Church. But I see now that the Church is on the offensive. The Church is moving against hell and the gates of hell cannot stand up against the Church.

That is what is represented in Revelation 12. The Devil is cast out of heaven. The Church is moving against the Devil. The Church will be victorious in the end. I'm sure that that is exactly what the verse in Matthew 18:18 means when Jesus said, "Whatsoever ye shall bind on earth shall be bound in heaven: and whatsoever ye shall loose on earth shall be loosed in heaven." This is referring to the second heaven and our spiritual activity in relationship to angels. Angels are responding to the faith of God's children.

14

Praise And Music

I have had the opportunity on several occasions over the last few years to minister at various Jesus festivals around America. About two years ago I was ministering at one of my favorite Jesus festivals outside of Washington, D.C., called Fishnet, when I met a young man from the West Coast that God is using in a powerful way. I had heard much about him and so I sat in to hear his message to the audience. What I heard shook me to the core. In fact, I had difficulty sleeping that night.

During his flight from the West Coast, he had sat next to the manager of one of the biggest rock-and-roll bands in the world. He said about the manager: "I was shocked at the intelligence of this man. He was a musical genius. I asked him a question, 'What do you think is next on the agenda for rock-and-roll? We are coming through the era of punk rock and new wave, where do we go from here?' "

Secular music's fourth phase

The manager of the rock band explained their strategy for the future. He said, "If you study rock music, it has gone through four phases. Each phase has appealed to one side of the human personality.

In the late 50's, early 60's, it appealed to sex entirely. In the late 60's going into the 70's, we tried to raise the consciousness and spiritual perception of young people. We were getting them involved in causes, Vietnam, etc. We opened them up to take drugs and experiment in other ways. We are now in the third era, the addictive rock-and-roll era. That is what punk rock is. Our music is violent and blaring. We don't feel quality is important. We are creating an addiciton to the sound of violence."

The manager continued, saying, "We're just like any other business. How do they sell cosmetics, clothes or cars? They find motivational triggers. We have discovered the best motivation to buy a product that there is in the world. It is religious commitment. *No human being ever makes a deeper commitment than a religious commitment.*

So we have decided that in the 80's we are going to have religious services in our concerts. We are going to pronounce ourselves as Messiah and we are going to make intimate acquaintances and covenants with Satan to pray for the sick and pull people out of wheel chairs during concerts. We will be worshipped."

When I heard those words, I was stunned. The secular music world is recognizing the power of the supernatural. They are beginning to move into that area of the supernatural and bring "healing" to their audiences.

What will the Church have to say to the next generation of young people? About two years ago a rock group had a huge concert outside of Toronto, Canada. At the end of their concert they gave what Christians would term an altar call, encouraging their audience to make covenants with the Devil. Several hundred responded.

If the world of secular music discovers the power of the supernatural and is able to combine the power of music and the supernatural, they will take the next generation. But where will the Church be in all of this? If the Church does not discover the power of praise and worship in music, and learn how to combine that with the supernatural, we will have no answer for what is coming in the days that lie ahead.

But I believe that God has an answer for the Church. I believe that God wants to prepare us, He wants us to be ready. God is not going to let demons have the final say in this generation. He is calling the Church to rise up, to enter into the authority that has been granted to it and to tear down the kingdom of Satan. Those demon spirits have to know that we're not going to let them go unchallenged. We're going to stand and declare war on the entire program of Satan.

Before we declare war, it is important to understand why he operates the way he does, we must get a perspective from the Word as to where his authority and power comes from. There are two classic Scriptural passages that deal with Satan in the Old Testament. Bible scholars generally agree that Ezekiel 28 and Isaiah 14 refer to the fall of Satan.

The perversion of music

In Ezekiel 28:13 a description of the Devil and his devices is given: "Thou has been in Eden the garden of God; every precious stone was thy covering … the workmanship of thy tabrets and of thy pipes was prepared in thee in the day that thou wast created." "The New American Standard Bible" (NASB) has changed "tabrets and pipes" to read "settings and sockets."

However, examination of the original Hebrew text verifies the translation as "tabrets and pipes." Even the

NASB has "tambourines and flutes" as an alternate
reading in the margin notes. Pipes would refer to wind
instruments in general. Tabrets or tambourines would
encompass the percussion instruments.

This verse describes some of the attributes and special abilities of the Devil. Satan, before his fall, had been
especially appointed to possess uniquely designed musical instruments, wind and percussion instruments.
Satan was obviously heaven's instrumentalist, able to
play both melody, and rhythm or percussion.

In Isaiah 14:11, another confirmation of Satan's musical prowess is given: "Thy pomp is brought down to
the grave, and the noise of thy viols." In "The New
King James Version" it reads, "Your pomp is brought
down to Sheol, And the sound of your stringed instruments."[1] Satan is accomplished in each of the major
areas of musical instruments: wind, strings, and percussion. Lucifer was obviously the master musician of
heaven.

This chapter says of Lucifer that he was a light-
bearer, or daystar. As a master musician, having innate
musical ability to create and play music, he would be
involved as the anointed Cherub covering the glory of
God with the music of heaven. I am sure Satan was involved at the creation of the earth, when the book of Job
38:7 says, "When the morning stars [or angels] sang together, and all the sons of God shouted for joy."

As the anointed Cherub that covered and as a master musician, it is highly probable that Lucifer led the
worship of heaven in covering the glory of God. But
Isaiah 14 tells us the story of his fall.

Sin entered into Satan's heart and he said, "I will
ascend into heaven, I will exalt my throne above the
stars of God." Lucifer took his eyes from the glory of

God and focused on his own beauty and brilliance. He was filled with pride. Instead of offering the worship to God that he was created for, he began to desire worship for himself.

Lucifer and one-third of the angels were cast out of the presence of God. Isaiah 14:12 describes Lucifer's fall. There is no indication that when he fell that his musical ability was taken away from him. When Lucifer fell, music fell with him.

His ability to create worship through music was perverted in the same way that his nature was perverted and turned against God. Music that was created for worship, created to fill the streets of glory, to ring throughout the ages in covering the glory of God, had now become tarnished. It became a tool Satan uses to raise people in rebellion against God. It began to appeal to the lower nature of man.

There's nothing in Scripture to indicate that Lucifer does not still have the ability to create music and to use it for his own nefarious purposes. He is using his false anointing now in secular music. He still has the powerful ability that will induce worship, but the worship is not directed to God the Father any longer. It is now directed to him.

Satan desires to be worshipped by mankind. The enemy knows God's primary desire for His children is for them to worship Him. Satan knows that if he is to be like God, he must divert the worship of mankind to himself.

That was the final temptation he placed before Jesus in the wilderness in Matthew 4:8-10, "Again, the devil taketh him up into an exceeding high mountain, and sheweth him all the kingdoms of the world, and the glory of them; And saith unto him, All these things will I give thee, if thou wilt fall down and worship me. Then saith Jesus unto him, Get thee hence, Satan: for it is written, Thou shalt worship the Lord thy God, and him only shalt thou serve."

Jesus did not contest the Devil's right to give him the kingdoms of the world. He did oppose him on the point of worship itself. Satan's desire was to get the worship of Jesus Christ. He knew that if Jesus would fall down and worship him that he would have attained the position of God the Father.

This is what is in the heart of Lucifer. But just because Satan failed, does not mean he is not offering the same type of arrangement to mankind today. Because of his unique ability to create music, he can offer a young, talented musician the same proposition that he gave to Jesus. He can offer them the kingdoms of this world. He can offer them fame, popularity, and money enough to blow the mind. He is influencing the music of our generation as an act of worship to himself and against God. He is inspiring those who do his music to lead large groups of people into making personal covenants with himself.

The importance of music

We must take a new look at this entire area of music and learn how to raise up music under God that will go forward in spiritual warfare to tear down the principalities and powers of the Devil. This is my strategy in my ministry. This is what I am doing with my Living Sound Teams. I am preparing them for this kind of onslaught. If the Devil is using music as the most important tool in capturing souls, then we must reexamine music to discover how to take souls with the power of God.

The day is past when we can intellectualize about

our music. The time has come for us to literally do warfare with our music. The time has come when praise and worship released through our music will do for us what it did for Jehoshaphat in the Old Testament.

Music is mentioned in the Bible over 800 times. It would do every believer good to notice the emphasis that Scripture places on the ways we are to respond to God and compare it to the fundamental doctrines outlined in Scripture.

The virgin birth is mentioned twice in the Bible, dancing five times, missions is mentioned twelve times, shouting commanded 65 times, justification is mentioned 70 times, thanksgiving 135 times, sanctification is mentioned 72 times, singing 287 times. Baptism is mentioned 80 times, rejoicing is commanded 288 times, repentance 110 times, playing musical instruments 317 times. Praise is mentioned and commanded 332 times.

This does not mean that the fundamental doctrines are not important; they give a structure to our faith that is absolutely necessary. *However, the preponderance of Scripture describes our response to God, not our doctrinal belief.* It is only natural to assume by this that God places great store in our response to Him, and music is one of the ways that God has commanded us to respond.

Psalm 100:2 says, "Come before his presence with singing." That is protocol. If we're going to come before the King of Kings, and Lord of Lords, we're to come singing. Music is important, the Father loves it.

God still requires the praise that is due Him. Because Lucifer is not there to lead the angels of heaven in covering the glory of God with praise and worship, God is determined to get it another way. He will get His praise and worship through the Church. He will get it through a race of beings who do not praise Him simply because of His command, but want to praise and worship the Lord, as an act of their own free will.

This redounds to the honor and glory of God in a much greater way than even the praise of angels. God has determined through the Church to cover that vacuum that exists in heaven. He *will* be glorfied.

Music in the Church

How does this translate into practical action for the Church today? What principles are there in Scripture that can give us a focus for our music in the Church? First of all, let's look at the Old Testament. Music in the house of God was particularly prominent in the reign of King David. David was a man after God's own heart because, more than anything else, David knew how to sing, and shout, and dance before the Lord.

The Bible indicates in 1 Chronicles 6:31-32 that David set priests and Levites in the house of the Lord for the sole purpose of providing music. They were to minister to God day and night with singing and instruments. It appears that they were full-time ministers of music, salaried by the tithes of the people. Notice 1 Chronicles 9:33, Nehemiah 11:2-23; 13:5. David recognized the importance of singing and praise in the tabernacle and that it should take place all the time.

This indicates the importance music should have in our church services today. Music was never meant to be just an ice-breaker or a warm-up exercise. Music is an important part of the relationship between God and His people.

David felt the musical instruments of his day were inadequate to manifest the music that was in his heart. So by God's inspiration, he designed and made musical instruments for the exclusive purpose of worshipping God (2 Chron. 7:6). Musical instruments have no ability in themselves to convey praise and worship. Their effectiveness depends upon the skill of the musician. There is musical ability within all of humanity. But musicians and singers have a special ability to communicate the message that God has given them through music.

Music was not created for evangelism. Neither was it created for secular purposes. Music was created for the worship of God. There is music in heaven covering the glory of God. This is thrilling the heart of God the Father. We should earnestly desire that this music of heaven should fill the earth. Didn't Jesus teach us to pray, "Thy will be done in earth even as it is in heaven?" *God's will for earth is praise and worship in the same way that it exists in heaven.*

Music and song has a tremendous ability to change attitudes and emotions within us. Can you imagine watching a television program with the music turned off? The sense of ebb-and-flow, of tension, is essentially created by the music. Music has the ability to mold and shape thoughts.

There are different kinds of music in the house of the Lord. In the Old Testament, there was definitely a prophetic song. It was a prophetic song that God gave to Moses in Deuteronomy 32:1-43. In the prophetic song the prophet is totally identified with God. Sometimes he speaks as though he is speaking, and sometimes God speaks in the first person through the prophet. There is a revelation element in the song that declares the purposes of God, His warnings, exhortations, and blessings. The prophetic song expresses the mind and heart of God.

There is a close connection between music and the prophetic. When Elisha needed to hear a word from the Lord for King Jehoshaphat, he called for the minstrel, a player of a stringed instrument, and asked him to play. Elisha could not prophesy until there was music and after the minstrel had played, the hand of the Lord came upon Elisha and gave him a prophetic utterance.

There is a unique connection between music and the spirit of the prophet. Often the spirit of prophecy will move through musicians more than anyone else in the church.

The music leaders of the Church need to be as anointed as the preachers. They need to have the Word of God in music, as much as the preacher. They need to be involved in pre-service prayer, waiting on the Lord, asking God what needs to be sung. God has a purpose and desire for every service. We gather to worship the King of Kings and the Lord of Lords.

Musicians are not to demonstrate their talent and to boost their egos, they are to submit and bow themselves before the Lord and use their talents as gifts of praise and worship unto the Father. There needs to be communication and unity between pastor and song leader, choir director, singers, and musicians.

The fact that the longest book in the Bible is a book of music seems to have escaped the attention of many believers in the Church. How many pastors give sufficient attention to the ministry of music and the worship of their Church? How many leaders of music truly have the desire to lead in music, truly to minister? Why is such scant attention given to Church music in many theological seminaries?

Martin Luther once said that music is second only to theology in the service of God. According to Luther,

"He who despises music does not please me. Music is a gift of God, not a gift of men. After theology, I accord it the highest place and the greatest honor."

Psalms, hymns and spiritual songs

There are three kinds of music believers should understand listed in Ephesians 5:17-20:

> 17 Wherefore be ye not unwise, but understanding what the will of the Lord is.
> 18 And be not drunk with wine, wherein is excess; but be filled with the Spirit;
> 19 Speaking to yourselves in psalms and hymns and spiritual songs, singing and making melody in your heart to the Lord;
> 20 Giving thanks always for all things unto God and the Father in the name of our Lord Jesus Christ.

Notice the three types of music mentioned here. Psalms, hymns, and spiritual songs. The Psalms were the hymn book of ancient Israel. There is something special about singing Psalms, especially when in spiritual warfare. The Psalms are the Word of God, written by David and others under the inspiration of the Holy Spirit. When we sing the Psalms, we are launching the weapon of the Word with the launching rocket of praise and worship. That is why the Psalms are being reintroduced to the Church today.

There is great spiritual energy released when a congregation begins to sing the Psalms. Many of the Psalms speak of the distress of the believer, but they always end with a message of hope. Let us learn again how to sing the Psalms.

Hymns are religious odes. In Deuteronomy 32, God inspired Moses to write a song intended for more than just his listeners as a temporary blessing, but one that was recorded and taught by one generation into the next. This is the description of the hymn. Hymns seem to convey the official message in song of the Church.

While the Psalms are more a celebration of God, hymns deal with the enduring themes, the eternal truths. Hymns like "Amazing Grace," or "How Great Thou Art" declare the goodness, the grace, and judgement of God. They possess a certain authority which other songs, though beautiful, do not contain.

Spiritual songs relate more to the subjective kind of singing that all of us do. Psalm 42:8 says, "in the night his song shall be with me." Psalm 32:7, "thou shalt compass me about with songs of deliverance." These special songs come from the influence of the Holy Spirit.

Perhaps this is what Paul refers to in 1 Corinthians 14:15, "I will sing with the spirit, and I will sing with the understanding also." When we sing in tongues we don't worry about rhyme or words, we are expressing deep feelings in the Spirit. When those moments come, the Spirit of prophecy can come upon us as well and we can pray with our understanding the words that we have prayed in the Spirit. These are spiritual songs, words of special ministry to us from the Lord.

Leading into the battle

It is impossible to overemphasize the importance of sensitivity to the Holy Spirit in the area of music. As we move into days of great spiritual warfare, there must be more singing and more instrumental music in the Church than ever before. Music is a vehicle through which God will express Himself to the Church. Through which the Church will express herself to God and to His people.

As we approach the time of the consummation of the ages, praise and worship are going to ascend to God with great power from the congregation of the blessed. We must be willing to abandon ourselves as musicians and instrumentalists to a place where the Holy Spirit can use us with great power.

I have listened as a pianist or organist was led in an anthem of worship. As the playing progressed, other instruments began to play under the same anointing, not following a score, but playing spontaneously in orchestral praise unto the Lord. This is spiritual warfare the way God wants it conducted. When we begin to move in this area, there will be miracles accomplished in the presence of believers.

The armies of the world march into battle with music and the Lord's army is no different. God is going to wage the warfare of this decade with those who will commit themselves to praise and worship. Notice how often music and instruments are associated with the great battles of God in the Old Testament, such as Joshua and the children of Israel marching around the walls of Jericho. They blew their trumpets, all the people gave a loud shout, and the walls of the city collapsed.

These stories have things to tell us. They reveal spiritual principles. Joshua was operating on the principle of spiritual warfare. There was a physical miracle with the collapse of the walls because the children of Israel were operating on the basis of spiritual principle. This is true of the battle that Jehoshaphat fought against the three invading armies.

The unified body

I have learned something important about the Church from Roman Catholic theology. Their ecclesiology refers to the Church in two parts. One part is described as the Church-militant. The other is referred to as the Church-triumphant. The Church-militant is the body of Christ around the earth; all believers in every nation of the earth. The Church-triumphant is that part of the body of Christ already gone on to be with the Lord. But they emphasize the importance of just one body, the Church-militant *and* the Church-triumphant as one. That means that part of the Church [the body] is before the throne of God offering worship to the Father.

I have come to appreciate this so much since I lost my wife. I know that Jan is in heaven. I know that she is before the throne of God covering the glory of God with her praise and worship. The Church-triumphant is encouraging the Church-militant to join them in praise and worship. The body must join together to give glory to God, in heaven, and on earth. "Thy will be done on earth as it is in Heaven."

---

[1] From *The New King James Version*. Copyright © 1979, 1980, 1982, Thomas Nelson, Inc., Publishers.

15

The Vow Of Praise

The story of David and Goliath has always been one of my favorites from the Old Testament. There's something special about little David facing big Goliath on the battlefield. Reading that victory of faith is a challenge to my spirit. Although I have preached the story of David and Goliath for years, I always had one question in my mind concerning the story which I had no answer for. *Where did David get the faith to face Goliath on the battlefield?*

Obviously, he was the only one in the nation who had faith. The soldiers of the army of Israel were terrified, as was Saul, their king. Yet, David was entirely unafraid to face Goliath. Where did that kind of faith come from? In preaching his story, I always illustrated the power of his faith and how his faith expressed itself, but I never could explain where that faith came from.

Awakened with the answer

In 1983, I was conducting a crusade in North Carolina and was staying in a motel. One morning I woke up suddenly at about 3:00 a.m. with an awareness that the Holy Spirit was speaking to me. I had not been meditating on the story of David and Goliath, but when I sat up in bed, I knew immediately that I had the answer.

I was impressed by the Holy Spirit to turn to the chapter preceding the story of David and Goliath, to 1 Samuel 16. I turned the light on at the head of my bed, opened my Bible and began to read through the chapter. What I read there made a lot of sense and I began to fully understand the story for the first time.

In 1 Samuel 16:14 it states, "But the Spirit of the Lord departed from Saul, and an evil spirit from the Lord troubled him." Saul had been disobedient to God. Samuel had commanded him to slay king Agag, the king of the Amalekites, which Saul had refused to do. Because of his disobedience to the Lord, the evil spirit began to trouble him. God simply permitted that evil spirit to operate. Apparently when the evil spirit disturbed him, he became unbearable.

So one day his servants came to him and said, "Saul, because you are so troubled by this evil spirit, why don't you find someone who is a cunning player on the harp, and perhaps when the evil spirit comes upon you, this man will play the harp and you will be well."

Saul thought it sounded like a good idea so he said to his servants, "Go and find someone who can play well and bring him to me." Apparently a talent search began at that point throughout Israel. Then one of his servants came one day and said, "Behold, I have seen a son of Jesse the Bethlehemite, that is cunning in playing, and a mighty valiant man, and a man of war, and prudent in matters, and a comely person, and the Lord is with him (16:18)." Saul sent messengers to Jesse and asked for David.

David was taking care of his father's sheep. He was spending time as a herdsman. He had also taken the time to become a cunning player on the harp. There is a tremendous message here for young people to practice and become good at their music. David spent all those years as a young boy, playing his harp and becoming good, never really aware of how his music would be useful in his life later on. As a boy with the sheep he would take his harp and play unto the Lord.

Some of the Psalms that were written and included in the book of Psalms were probably written by David while he was a teenage boy taking care of his father's sheep. The Bible says that David came to Saul and stood before him, and Saul loved him greatly, and he became his armor bearer.

When the evil spirit was upon Saul, David took his harp, played with his hand and Saul was refreshed and the evil spirit departed from him. This is spiritual warfare. This is a unique reference in Scripture. It correlates exactly with the words that David wrote in Psalm 8:1, 2, "O Lord our Lord, how excellent is thy name in all the earth! who hast set thy glory above the heavens. Out of the mouth of babes and sucklings hast thou ordained strength because of thine enemies, that thou mightest still the enemy and the avenger."

Praise stills the enemy and the avenger. It tells the Devil to shut up. The Devil cannot harass any longer. His power to control is destroyed. Praise has this effect upon the Devil. David wrote Psalm 8 based on his experience with King Saul. He had seen praise drive an evil spirit out of King Saul.

Praise is the key to power

As a boy, spending time taking care of his father's sheep, David learned the power of praise. He learned how to flow in praise to the Lord. He learned the importance that praise has in a believer's heart. David was later called the man after God's own heart. More than anything else David knew how much God wanted the praise of His people. So he was prepared to give Him that praise. *This is the key to David's power.* This is where David got the faith to face Goliath.

The stronger the faith, the more reverberating the praise becomes. The stronger the praise, the more reverberating the faith becomes. Praise is more than a casual point of contact, more than a cure-all, more than a formula for manipulating the Word of God. *Praise is the generator for a powerful faith.*

Faith moves us and launches us into an area where we begin to actively apply the Word of God. You cannot move in praise without faith being present and motivating that act of praise. Praise is like the trigger that releases the explosion of faith. Our application of praise in faith will cause the Word to come alive.

Many times praise will be a celebration of triumph. We will thank God for the completed work of Calvary, even before we see in someone's life the demonstration of that finished work. We may need healing and we praise God for the fact that healing has been accomplished, even before we have seen the physical results or manifestations in our own life.

We must be very careful at this point. *We cannot make praise a source for the manipulation of God. It is not a coin in a cosmic vending machine.* But according to Scripture, it is absolutely correct to praise God for expected results and promises on the basis of the law of faith.

To passively sit back and accept whatever happens in our life reduces the Christian soldier to a spiritual baby being dominated by circumstance. We grow into maturity by exercising the authority and dominion Jesus delegated to us before He left the earth.

Someone has said, prayer asks but praise takes. Prayer talks about the problem, but praise takes the answer from God. The time to praise God is when the pressure is the greatest, when the valley is the darkest. That's when praise releases faith.

A commitment of praise

David was continually offering praise unto God. Psalms 61:8 states, "So will I sing praise unto thy name for ever, that I may daily perform my vows." *It is clear that David had made a vow that he would daily praise the Lord.* Everyday of his life David was committed to praise, and it is obvious that his daily vow of praise had built an incredible faith. His confrontation with Goliath was the demonstration of that faith.

The Philistines had invaded the land of Israel. The two armies were pitched on opposite sides of a valley. Everyday for 40 days the Philistine's champion, Goliath, had marched into the valley and challenged the armies of Israel. He said, "I defy the armies of Israel this day; give me a man, that we may fight together. If he be able to fight with me, and to kill me, then will we be your servants: but if I prevail against him, and kill him, then shall ye be our servants, and serve us." Saul and all Israel were dismayed and greatly afraid.

Jesse, David's father, came to David one morning and suggested that he take some food to his brothers. David's three older brothers were fighting with the king. David took the food and went to the battle line and arrived just as the armies were preparing to line-up in the valley. David ran through the hosts and greeted his brothers.

As he was talking to Eliab, his oldest brother, he heard this mighty roar down in the valley. He went to the top of the hill and saw the biggest man he had ever seen in his life. Goliath stood in the valley nine feet, nine inches tall (6 cubits and a span). David noticed that all the men of Israel were afraid when they saw Goliath. But David's reaction was immediate and simple. He said, "Who is this uncircumcised, Philistine that he should defy the armies of the living God?"

That kind of reaction in a teenage boy is surprising. David's faith talk is amazing. Where did he learn this? From taking care of his father's sheep, playing his harp, and practicing his vow unto the Lord. This kind of faith had grown out of David's praise. *When you are a person of praise, you will talk the talk of faith.* It will not be the boastful talk of ego. It will be the talk of simple faith in God.

Notice who was the first one to attack David's faith — his oldest brother. No one can rob you of faith more quickly than someone in your own family. They know your weaknesses, they know your problems, and their scorn can turn you from faith faster than anything else.

Eliab came and accused David of shooting off his mouth. Eliab was embarrassed by what the young David was saying. Eliab said, "All you are is a sheep herder, and you've just come down so you might see the battle. Now you're shooting your mouth off. Why don't you go back and take care of the sheep?"

But the Bible records that David turned from his brother and spoke in the same manner to another man. David would not change the confession of his faith. *He had been a person of praise too long to change his words of faith.* Faith was a part of his spirit. The boy could not think any other way.

David was summoned to the tent of King Saul. We have a classic picture at this point of David, the young man of faith, standing before the military tribunal of

Saul, the king of Israel. All the chiefs are sitting behind a table. David walks in, salutes Saul, and Saul ridicules him and says, "David you can't do it. You are but a youth and Goliath is a man of war from his youth." Then David tells Saul about the lion and the bear.

Where did a teenage boy learn to kill a lion and a bear with his bare hands? David certainly had been learning what faith was like as he praised the Lord and exercised his daily vow of praise unto the Lord. Something had happened in his spirit that had made him a powerful man of God. Saul was so overwhelmed at the confidence of the young David that he finally encouraged him to face Goliath.

Praise had built something into the faith of the boy. He could not talk fear. He could not talk defeat. He could only talk the power of God that was flowing through him.

The next challenge to David's confession is on the battlefield against Goliath. When Goliath saw the boy coming to him, he got very upset. He said, "Am I a dog, that thou comest to me with staves?" Now David is entering into spiritual warfare. David was a man of God coming against an enemy controlled by strongholds.

Goliath cursed David by his gods, gods that were really demon spirits. Those gods were spirits that David already had dealt with. David had dealt with that demon spirit that filled King Saul. That spirit had had to leave and depart from the king. Saul had been refreshed by the praise of David. David knew how to take care of the demon spirits that were controlling Goliath the Philistine.

Goliath said to David, "Come to me and I will give thy flesh unto the fowls of the air, and unto the beasts of the field." Notice the confession of David and his words as he comes against the greatest military champion of his day.

David said, "Thou comest to me with a sword, and with a spear, and with a shield: *but I come to thee in the name of the Lord of hosts.*" That is the key. David was not only a person of praise, but he had learned that praise launches spiritual weapons. *David understood the power of the Name.*

David knew that the power of God is represented in His Name. So he said to Goliath, "You come to me with instruments of war, but I come to you in spiritual warfare. I come to you in the power of the Name. I bind the stronghold that motivates you. I bind the stronghold that gives you strength and I am coming to you in the power of that Name."

Giant-killing faith

Then in 1 Samuel 17:46, 47, David states boldly, "This day will the Lord deliver thee into mine hand; and I will smite thee, and take thine head from thee; and I will give the carcases of the host of the Philistines this day unto the fowls of the air, and to the wild beasts of the earth; that all the earth may know that there is a God in Israel. And all this assembly shall know that the Lord saveth not with sword and spear: for the battle is the Lord's, and he will give you into our hands."

What a statement of faith! What power resided in that young man. What praise had done for him, praise can do for all of us. *Praise builds that kind of faith into the human spirit.* Praise moves us to that kind of a confrontational situation. We will see healing, we will see deliverence, we will see marriages turned around. We will see financial victories through people who are flowing in faith, to this degree.

The Bible says David ran to meet Goliath. He put his hand into his bag, took a stone, and he slung it, and smote Goliath in the forehead. Goliath fell with a mighty crash. David stood on top of him, cut off his head with his own sword, and Israel won a great victory.

You cannot help but be overwhelmed with the connection of faith and praise in this story. Giant-slaying faith comes from praise. Praise prepares you for the miracle-working power of God. But this praise is not a random little, "I thank You Lord", once or twice in a Sunday morning service. This kind of praise comes from a vow.

The vow of daily praise

David's vow in Psalm 61:8 is an excellent model for our own vows of praise: "So will I sing praise unto thy name for ever, that I may daily perform my vows."

First, David states, "So *will* I sing." The will is involved. David says he *will* praise the Lord, not that he's going to praise the Lord when and if he feels like it. And this must be our attitude toward praise. I will sing even when I'm down. I will sing even when I don't want to. I will sing even when things are going wrong. David had learned the power of the sacrifice of praise.

In Psalm 34 when he wrote, "I will bless the Lord at all times: his praise shall continually be in my mouth," he was in exile, running from the anger of King Saul. He had fled to the land of the Philistines. He was dwelling with Abimilech in the city of Gath. Abimilech suspected David of being a traitor, so David had to act like a madman. He would stand at the wall with spittle running down his beard, scrabbling like an insane man on the wall.

In the midst of this kind of terror, this kind of fear, David wrote Psalm 34. I will bless the Lord at all times. I will bless the Lord when I'm forced to act like a madman. I will bless the Lord when the enemy is about to destroy me. His praise shall continually be in my mouth.

This is a vow. The boy was remembering his vow even in his old age. *So will I sing.* David's will was involved and his praise was manifested in singing. David wrote much about singing. In Psalm 100 he wrote, "Make a joyful noise unto the Lord ... come before his presence with singing." David knew the importance of singing as an expression of the soul to God.

In Psalm 55:17, David said, "and he shall hear my voice." There is something about the voice that gives power to praise. David says in Psalms 65:1, "Praise waiteth for thee, O God, in Sion: and unto thee shall the vow be performed." Again David makes a reference to his vow of praise.

In Psalms 35:28, he states, "My tongue shall speak of thy righteousness and of thy praise all the day long." David was overwhelmed with the power of praise. He was totally committed to that kind of praise all day long.

This is the key to the power of David's spiritual life. David understood the principles of spiritual warfare. He knew that the powerful weapon that God had given him was the Name. Praise was the launching rocket that would take the Name and apply it against the Devil. So he says, "So will I sing praise unto Thy name."

Remember, it was the Name that David mentioned against Goliath as he came against him. He said, "I come to thee in the name of the Lord of hosts." Praise

God for the power of His Name.

This is an eternal commitment on David's part. I'm sure that right now as you read this book, David is praising God in heaven. He is standing in front of the throne playing his harp. He is singing the song of a soul set free, the song of the redeemed. David is singing praise to His Name forever.

Next in Psalm 61:8, David states, "that I may *daily* perform my vows." Proverbs 8:34 says, "Blessed is the man that heareth me, watching daily at my gates, waiting at the post of my doors." Psalm 72:15 says, "and daily shall he be praised." *God desires a consistent commitment of praise.*

Praise was not optional with David. It was crucial. He had learned the key of its power and vowed to praise God on a daily basis, everyday of his life. Psalm 22:25 proclaims, "My praise shall be of thee in the great congregation: I will pay my vows before them that fear him." David is proclaiming his vow of praise in the midst of the congregation. He wants the people to know how important a function praise is in his life.

In Psalm 116:18, 19, David declares further, "I will pay my vows unto the Lord now in the presence of all his people, In the courts of the Lord's house, in the midst of thee, O Jerusalem. Praise ye the Lord."

The importance of vows

A vow is a promise. Scripture indicates that religious vows were regarded with great seriousness in the sight of God. The Nazarites were required to make special vows to God. Samson and John the Baptist were Nazarites. Hannah made a vow that Samuel would be the servant of the Lord.

Solomon writes in the book of Ecclesiastes 5:4,

"When thou vowest a vow unto God, defer not to pay it [don't be late in paying]; for he hath no pleasure in fools: pay that which thou hast vowed." When we make a promise to God, the Scripture says we must live up to it. Ecclasiastes 5:5 says you'd be better if you didn't vow at all than to vow and not pay your vow.

Our religious commitments are not taken lightly in the sight of God. David knew that his vow was sacred. He knew the importance of the vow. We have forgotten the importance of that vow in contemporary Christianity. But David knew if he had made a vow to daily praise the Lord, that this had to become a lifestyle; a commitment that was more important to him than life itself.

When I was traveling with a group from Oral Roberts University in 1968, and we ventured behind the Iron Curtian, I was stirred by the commitment of the Soviet Christians. Attending a secret meeting of an underground church, I made a vow that I would readily minister in the Soviet Bloc if God called me to. Two years later, as I've described earlier in this book, God did call me. I was required to make good on my vow.

That vow has become the foundation for my ministry to date. As I write these words, I am in a Soviet Bloc country. I am conducting crusades in the heart of Poland. Tomorrow we will be in the home church of Lech Walesa, the leader of Solidarity in Poland. In a few days my team will depart for a very sensitive mission into the Soviet Union. Today I am paying my vow. I told the Lord that I would do it and He has called me. It is not something that I am allowed to take lightly.

So it was with David. He said, "So will I sing praise unto thy name for ever, that I may daily perform my vow." In this business of praise we do not accept or respond because it sounds like a plausible doctrine. We don't really have an option. We are commanded by God to praise Him. It is obvious the faith of David grew out of his vow of praise.

It is incumbent upon every Christian to make the vow of praise unto God. No one can force you into it. No one can manipulate you to do it. But in order to be moving in faith of the magnitude of David's, we must come to a place where praise is a daily function.

Hebrews 13:15 states, "By him therefore [or through Christ] let us offer the sacrifice of praise to God continually, that is, the fruit of our lips giving thanks to his name." That is the New Testament counterpart of what David did in the Old Testament. It is the New Testament understanding of the power of praise in the life of an Old Testament hero. The necessity for making a vow of praise is as important for us today as it was for David then.

16

Praising The Lord

As I travel around the United States, Canada and other parts of the world, there is one question that I am continually asked: "How should we lead our congregations in praise and worship? How can we actually engage in thanksgiving, praise, and worship and come into the presence of almighty God? Is there any kind of Scriptural design that we can follow?"

I believe there is. In Psalm 100 we have the divine pattern for entering in to the presence of God. We are encouraged in verse one of the Psalm to make a joyful noise unto the Lord. In verse two we are encouraged to come before His presence with singing. This Psalm represents the habits of the Old Testament Hebrews.

They were accustomed to singing as they journeyed up to Jerusalem to celebrate the feast days. They had a series of psalms that were sung. These were called the Psalms of Ascent, or degrees. You will find them in the book of Psalms, 120-134. As they approached Jerusalem for the special religious festival, they would begin to sing the Psalms before they ever came to the temple.

The singing prepared their hearts for the worship they would be involved in when they arrived at the temple. It stirred their faith, and it brought their hearts and minds together in worship unto the Lord.

Notice where the Psalms of Ascent start; Psalm 120:1, "In my distress I cried unto the Lord, and he heard me." And notice where the Psalms of Ascent end; Psalms 134:2, "Lift up your hands in the sanctuary, and bless the Lord." They begin with man's problem, with man's distress and difficulties, and they end with man in the presence of God in the sanctuary.

Focusing on God

David gives us an overview of the Psalms of Ascents in Psalm 100. He echoes the voice of the people as they come up toward Jerusalem, as they sing to one another; "Make a joyful noise unto the Lord, all ye lands. Serve the Lord with gladness: come before his presence with singing." In that phrase you have the protocol of coming before the King of Kings.

Earlier I discussed protocol and how God demands that we come before Him. We come into His presence with singing, with praise and worship. It is uncertain where the song service as we know it came from. But it is probable that it came out of this pattern in the Old Testament of the people singing on their way up to the tabernacle. On their way into the presence of God they prepared their hearts with thanksgiving, praise and worship.

It is important that we see the role that singing has in providing the unity in the hearts of the people and preparing them for the act of worship before God.

Singing in our song services prepares us for worship. If the people will give their hearts completely to the leadership of the Holy Spirit in the meeting, no matter what the concerns of their day have been, no matter how distressing the affairs of business, or household chores, they will be successful.

Singing provides a flow of unity that allows a focus for believers to flow together in coming before the Lord. And so it is the job of the songleader to gather the scattered thoughts of the congregation and begin to focus them on God with music.

There are many choruses in most hymnals that relate to this particular situation. The Psalmist writes in Psalms 100:1, "Make a joyful noise unto the Lord," and that is where we begin, with a joyful noise. The important factor is to bring the people into a unity of spirit.

In Psalm 120, in the Psalms of Ascent, the people are very much concerned with their personal distresses, their personal problems. In Psalm 121 they quickly arrive at, "I will lift up mine eyes unto the hills from whence cometh my help." They are preparing to come into the tabernacle. They know they cannot come into the actual experience of worship until they are in the tabernacle itself.

This is important to remember for any songleader. We can involve ourselves in a lot of singing that takes place outside the "tabernacle" in getting people ready, but this is not necessarily worship. Unless there is an actual plan and design to the song service, it will never lead the people into the presence of God and into the act of worship.

The focus, the end result of any song service must be worship. The plan is to bring the congregation, to bring the people, into the presence of the Lord. Ultimately, into the Holy of Holies. So we find ourselves walking through the tabernacle. I have found the tabernacle to be an excellent design and pattern for the worship of the believer.

Entering God's presence

The writer to the Hebrews describes the importance of the design of the tabernacle in Hebrews 9:1-9. He describes the various items of furniture in the tabernacle and then makes an unusual statement in verse 8: "The Holy Ghost this signifying, [was showing, by the Old Testament tabernacle] that the way into the holiest of all [into the actual presence of God] was not yet made manifest, while as the first tabernacle was yet standing." The Holy Ghost has a plan in the tabernacle that wasn't really made manifest while the original tabernacle was standing.

In other words, there is a pattern, a model in the tabernacle that we can follow today. The way into the holiest of all is the way of worship. God dwells in the Holy of Holies, the holiest of all. The tabernacle shows us the pattern to get to the holiest of all. In this chapter we will consider the design of the tabernacle and the various items of furniture, and show how a song service can lead people into the actual presence of God for worship.

In the diagram shown on the last page of this chapter, there are illustrated the three areas of the tabernacle. There are several ways of looking at the three areas of the tabernacle. They can represent many things.

The outer court: the body

First, the outer court represents the body of man. The holy place represents the soul of man, composed of his mind, his will and his emotions. The Holy of Holies refers to the spirit of man. God is a spirit and we must worship Him in spirit and in truth. So in the tabernacle you see man coming from the conscious awareness of his body, through the various elements of his soul, into a place of worship in the spirit with God.

The outer court also stands for our thanksgiving as it relates more to the body. The holy place relates to the soul, and praise relates us to the elements of the soul. Worship of course is offered in the Holy of Holies, in the presence of God, in the presence of the shekinah, and takes place in the human spirit. And so as we walk through the tabernacle, we take the three steps necessary for divine worship: thanksgiving, praise, and worship.

Psalm 100:4 says we must come through the gate of the outer court of the tabernacle with thanksgiving. Remember that thanksgiving relates to what God has done for us. When we begin to recount the great deeds of God in our past: when we were saved, when we were baptized with the Holy Spirit, when God ministered to us and performed miracles financially, when we saw healing in the lives of our children, or in those that were dear to us, we prepare ourselves.

Then we must thank God for those great things that He has done. Not only in His actual deeds or miracles but also what He has done for us spiritually, through the act of salvation. He has given us His righteousness. We now have no condemnation as we stand before Him. Healing has been provided for us in the atonement. Financial blessings flow to us as we stand in His promises of prosperity. The focus of these kinds of songs brings the people into an attitude of thanksgiving.

The outer court represents the body of man and this is where the body of man gets involved in the process of thanksgiving, praise, and worship. Psalms 100:4 says enter into His gates with thanksgiving. The word for thanksgiving there is *towdah,* in Hebrew. Enter into His courts with praise is *tehillah.*

Towdah and its root *yadah* mean to revere or worship with extended hands. It involves the lifting of the hands. Raising our hands is an act of humility and surrender of the flesh. It is an act of the body. Our body must be brought into submission in the outer court.

The act of thanksgiving should inspire the physical acts that often accompany worship. It should be in thanksgiving that we begin to clap our hands. It is in thanksgiving that we dance before the Lord. It is with thanksgiving that we play the timbrels. We come with shouting, with gladness. By clapping our hands and shouting with a voice of triumph. This is what thanksgiving does. Thanksgiving involves the human body in an act of a sacrifice (Psalms 33:3, 47:1, 86:12, 89:1, 95:1, 144:9).

We begin to sacrifice with thanksgiving before we move to the sacrifice of praise. Our body is commanded to submit itself in an act of sacrifice to God. This relates directly to Romans 12:1, "I beseech you therefore, brethren, by the mercies of God, that ye present your bodies a living sacrifice, holy, acceptable unto God, which is your reasonable service." This is coming into the outer court. This is presenting our bodies as a sacrifice on the altar.

Putting our lives on the altar

The first item of furniture in the outer court was the huge brazen altar. It was seven-and-a-half feet square. It was situated squarely in the opening entrance to the outer court. It was on this altar that the priests shed the blood of the innocent sacrifice. The blood was carried from that altar by the high priest on the day of atonement into the Holy of Holies.

This was the act of sacrifice. This is where our bodies must be placed. According to Paul in Romans 12, we lay our bodies as a living sacrifice on that altar. This happens when we enter into the act of a sacrifice of thanksgiving. Our bodies actually are placed upon the altar of God. This is the reasonable, the sensible thing for us to do. We are on our way into the Holy of Holies to worship the Lord.

Cleansing our bodies

The second item of furniture in the outer court was the brazen laver. This was a large bowl filled with water. The bowl was made from the brass mirrors of the women of Israel. When you looked into the water, you could see your reflection in the brass. This refers to the Word of God. This indicates the washing of water by the Word according to Ephesians 5:26 and Hebrews 10:22. It is important that our bodies be cleansed by the washing of the Word.

We must find songs of thanksgiving that relate to the power of the Word, that relate to the great deeds that God has done for us. When we begin to sing the Word, we release a special spiritual power against the strongholds that would bind our bodies.

The holy place: the soul

As our bodies are being brought into submission, we prepare ourselves to take the next step outlined in our pattern chapter, Psalm 100. Now we come into His courts with praise. The word for praise here is *tehillah*. *Tehillah* means to sing *halals*. The word *halal*, the root word for hallelujah, means to make a show, to boast, to be clamorously foolish, to rave, to celebrate. Therefore, *tehillah* means to sing *halals*, to sing praises extravagantly, to celebrate with song.

This is how we come into His courts with praise. We come into His courts with a kind of extravagant singing and boastful praise.

It is important to note that *once we move to songs of praise, we ought to stay with praise, and not revert to songs of thanksgiving.* Many song leaders inadvertently lead people from the outer court into the holy place and back to the outer court again. We must understand the focus of the outer court, the holy place, and eventually the Holy of Holies.

The songs of praise will ultimately focus on the character of God. They will extol Him for His goodness. "I will sing of the mercies of the Lord forever. I will sing." They will focus on who He is and the wonders of His presence in our lives.

Notice how the pattern moves us from the distress we felt as we came up to the house of the Lord. Then into thanksgiving to God for His great deeds in our past. When we get our minds off of distress and problems, and begin to focus on what God has already done for us, the wheels of our faith begin to roll. We are preparing for a miracle.

Praise takes us one step past the deeds that God has done in the past and begins to focus us on who God is to us now. This is where our heart prepares itself for miracles. We are willing to believe that God can do now what He has done in the past. We move through that subtle transition of thanksgiving into the area of praise.

Sacrificing our wills

When we move into the holy place in the tabernacle there are three items of furniture that we must note. The first item of furniture is the table of shewbread. On top of that table there are twelve loaves of bread, freshly baked. They are lined in two rows of six. The shewbread represents the will of man in the human personality. We have now moved into the area of man's soul.

Praise comes forth from the soul of man. I have previously dealt with the importance of praise relating to the will of man. Praise is not an act of our emotions, although the emotions ultimately become involved with praise. Praise begins with an act of the will. We decide to put on a garment of praise for the spirit of heaviness. This is where the sacrifice of praise that Paul and Silas offered in the Philippian jail relates to the will.

The bread is significant in typifying the human will. When we make bread, the first thing we do is grind the wheat into flour. This is what must happen to the human will. When we are on our way into the presence of God, we must submit our will unto God. We must decide to praise the Lord. Jesus said, "My meat (or my food) is to do the will of Him that sent me."

The next step in making bread is to put it in the fire for baking. Our wills go through the fire of difficulty and testing and in so doing are submitted completely to the will of God.

Jesus said to the Father in the garden of Gethsemane, "not my will, but thine, be done." This takes place as an act of submission on our way into the Holy of Holies. The will is submitted unto the Lord. We begin to praise the Lord as an act of sacrifice no matter how difficult the testings of life no matter how hot the furnace and the fire have been. This moves us to the point of the sacrifice of praise.

Illuminating our minds

The second item of furniture in the holy place is the seven-branched golden candlestick or lampstand. At the top of each branch is a bowl of burning oil. This candlestick is the only means of light in the holy place.

The candlestick represents the human mind; a human mind that is illuminated by the fire of the Holy Spirit. Once again we are reminded of what Paul writes in Romans 12:2. After we have made a living sacrifice of our bodies, then we do not become conformed to this world, but we are to be transformed by the renewing of our mind.

One of the great means God uses in renewing the human mind is the power of the prayer language in the life of the believer. After the will has been submitted through the sacrifice of praise, we find ourselves flowing in the power of our prayer language.

As we begin to sing in the spirit as a congregation, there is a powerful involvement of the Holy Spirit in the act of praise. We are going through the active process of the renewing of our minds. Our minds are being prepared for the act of worship. Our minds are being submitted to the Lordship of Jesus Christ. It is exactly at this point that spiritual warfare is transacted.

Remember the primary scripture of this book; "For the weapons of our warfare are not carnal, but mighty through God to the pulling down of strongholds" (2 Cor. 10:4). Strongholds bind us in the area of thought. Imaginations must be cast down, "every high thing that exalts itself against the knowledge of God." Every thought is to be brought into captivity to the mind of Christ.

When we flow in our prayer language, we are giving preeminence to the Spirit. We are entering into the act of spiritual warfare. We are beginning to think the thoughts of God. Our mind is being renewed by the Holy Spirit. The strongholds that the enemy has created in us must be pushed out of the way as we begin to flow in the divine thoughts of God.

The prayer language releases us into the power of spiritual warfare. The will has submitted itself for the sacrifice of praise. The mind has submitted itself to the flow of the Holy Spirit. We are actively involved in casting down imaginations. Every thought is being brought into the captivity of the mind of Christ. We have prepared ourselves for a miracle and we can begin to expect it from the hand of almighty God.

Releasing our emotions

The third item of furniture in the holy place is the golden altar of incense. Every time a high priest came into the holy place, he was to take a handful of this special incense and sprinkle it upon the living coals on that altar. The resulting cloud of perfumed smoke permeated the linen veil that separated the presence of the shekinah glory of God from the priests. It saturated the clothing of the priest with the fragrance of the sacrificial incense.

This altar represents the human emotions. When the will has been submitted to a sacrifice of praise, the mind has been submitted to the Holy Spirit in the flow of the prayer language, then there is a powerful flow of the emotions.

The emotions do not dictate our praise in the holy place. The will does that. The mind follows suit, and as our mind is brought under the subjection of the Holy Spirit, our emotions give powerful and intense expression through the praise of our lips and our heart. It is that emotional thrust that brings us through the veil into the act of worship.

We should never be ashamed of our emotions in this context as long as they are kept in place. It is at the golden altar of incense that a sacrificial fragrance rises up into the nostrils of God and makes Him well pleased. This is the final step that we take before we move through the veil into the presence of His shekinah glory. Incense was very costly. This speaks of the sacrifice that praise represents in the subjection of the human soul to the flow of the Spirit of God.

The most holy place: the spirit

The believer will not always enter into the Holy of Holies. This is the ideal for the believer coming into the presence of God. Sometimes a congregation will stop with thanksgiving. Sometimes it will move on into praise, then into the high praise that takes place and transpires at the altar of incense.

There is something sovereign, however, in the invitation to worship. We bring ourselves to a point where our bodies and minds have been subjected, but *we await the divine invitation of God to actually come into His presence.*

When that invitation is given, the song leader must be very sensitive to it. He should not ruin that special moment by misspeaking or misdirecting the service. When that moment happens, it is electric. It is the *now* moment of God's Holy Spirit. A congregation must be taught to respond to that moment, and to collectively move in at the invitation of the Lord.

In the presence of God

In some of my meetings across America, I have seen this special moment happen, without a sign from anyone, I have watched an entire congregation get down on its knees. I have seen them lay on the floor with an overwhelming sense of the presence and power of almighty God. At other times the people have gone into a hushed silence.

There is no way of programing that moment of worship. It is the invitation of the Holy Spirit and we must be very sensitive to it.

There must also be a sensitivity when the time of worship is over, and it may be necessary to choose one more chorus to bring the audience back into the outer court in preparation for the ministry of the Word. There may be times in the moment of worship when an altar call should be given. Sensitivity is vital.

Because the Lord has instructed me to bring His people into salvation, healing, and deliverance, through praise and worship, I will often interrupt the service in the midst of high praise and conduct a healing service. I will direct the faith of the people toward the supernatural miracles of God. I encourage them to believe for those miracles, and invariably I have seen in every service miracles of one sort or another. However, this is not the supreme good for this kind of service.

Ultimately, the focus of the service must be worship. We must extravagantly pour ourselves out as the woman broke the alabaster bottle and poured it out on the feet of Jesus. We must pour ourselves out before the Lord. This is the purpose of praise and worship. The miracles that God brings in the holy place are simply the attendant signs.

The end result for every believer must be the entrance into the presence of God in worship. Being in the presence of God is the greatest miracle of all.

The Tabernacle

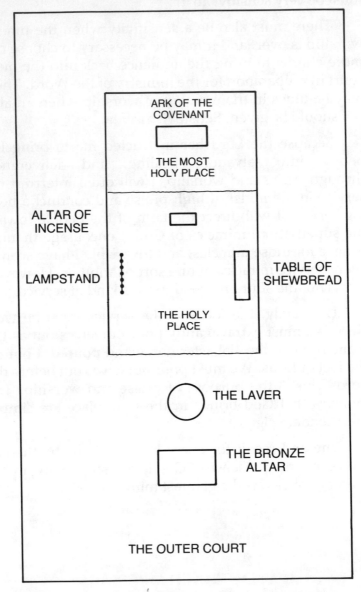

ARK OF THE
COVENANT

THE MOST
HOLY PLACE

ALTAR OF
INCENSE

LAMPSTAND

TABLE OF
SHEWBREAD

THE HOLY
PLACE

THE LAVER

THE BRONZE
ALTAR

THE OUTER COURT

About the Author

Terry Law, president and founder of Terry Law Ministries, has become one of America's foremost speakers on Praise and Worship.

In the late 1960's, Terry Law began an international missionary team called Living Sound. With a special emphasis in world missions, he has led Living Sound teams to minister in over forty countries of the world, seeing multiplied thousands of people accept Jesus Christ as Savior. His work continues through Living Sound Europe, Living Sound Russia, and Living Sound Poland.

Terry and his wife, Shirley, and their six children reside in Tulsa, Oklahoma. Through his world headquarters in Tulsa, he coordinates the multi-faceted outreaches of the ministry and ministers worldwide in the areas of Praise and Worship and missions with a special emphasis on healing.

For a complete list of tapes and books by Terry Law, including the following new releases:

Praise Releases Faith
by Terry Law
and
Yet Will I Praise Him
by Terry and Shirley Law

write to:
LAW OUTREACH MINISTRIES
P.O. Box 3563
Tulsa, Oklahoma 74101

Books by Terry Law
Available From Victory House

Praise Releases Faith
_____

The Power Of Praise And Worship
_____

Your Spiritual Weapons
_____

How To Overcome Guilt
_____

How To Overcome Giants
_____

How To Enter The Presence Of God
_____

Victory House
P.O. Box 700238 ● Tulsa, OK. 74170